The Doctrine of Anarchism

of

Michael A. Bakunin

The Doctrine of
ANARCHISM
of
Michael A. Bakunin

By Eugene Pyziur

A Gateway Edition

The Henry Regnery Company • Chicago

Library of Congress Catalog Card Number: 55-12423

Copyright, 1955, Marquette University Press, Milwaukee, Wis.

First Gateway edition, 1968

IN MEMORIAM IRENAE

Contents

The Doctrine of
ANARCHISM

CHAPTER 1

BAKUNIN'S PERSONALITY

In HIS article on communism printed in 1843 in *Der Schweizerische Republikaner*, Bakunin wrote:

We were born under the star of revolution and we shall all, without exception, die under its influence. We are on the eve of a great universal historical upheaval, which will be the more dangerous since it will have not only a political but also a dogmatic and religious character.[1]

As for Bakunin himself, this prediction was certainly fulfilled completely. In the revolutionary firmament of the 19th century, his star was one of the brightest. His revolutionary performance was unprecedented, for he was not only a leading actor but also his own stage manager and scenario writer. In his performances, he usually, though not always, had a small supporting cast, but he reduced its members to supernumeraries. His lifelong friend, the famous Russian radical, Herzen, once remarked: "This man was born not under an ordinary star, but under a comet."[2]

A member of a Russian aristocratic family, Bakunin gave up the career and way of life of this social class and soon identified himself with a new social group which was then emerging in Russia, the intelligentsia. In Moscow, in the discussion groups of this new class, he discovered German philosophy, and at once became a great enthusiast. The desire to deepen his self-taught knowledge led him to the University of Berlin. There he soon, though not for long, approached the position of the left Hegelians. However, he quickly became disappointed in philosophy, though he never was to be able to resist his impulse toward philosophizing; he gave up his plans for a career as a scholar, and plunged wholeheartedly into the revolutionary movement

[1] M. A. Bakunin, *Sobraniye sochinenii i pisem*, Steklov ed., III, 230.
[2] D. I. Chizhevski, *Gegel v Rossii* (Paris, 1939), p. 84.

of his time. For the rest of his eventful life, he devoted himself to the making of revolution. But at the very beginning of his revolutionary career, he discovered that none of the contemporary revolutionary doctrines afforded a sufficient ideological basis for a revolution of such dimensions as that which he planned. This led him to create his own ideological premises for his concept of revolution. At first, he raised the banner of "revolutionary Pan-Slavism." When this proved insufficient to take the hinges off the existing world, Bakunin, who had felt an increasing solidarity with the working class movement, created his own conception of anarchism to which he remained faithful to the end of his days.

This was Bakunin's political-ideological development. Against the backdrop of these rapid ideological changes, the almost exotic adventures and events of Bakunin's life unfolded. His life was like a work of fiction, and attracted many who were completely indifferent to Bakunin's political strivings. In Russian literature alone we find Bakunin's portrait in novels by Ivan Turgenev and Roman Gul, in the poetry of Ivan Aksakov, and in the dramas of Dmitri Mereshkovski and Konstantin Fedin.[3] Shortly after World War I, there was a long discussion among Russian literary critics as to whether Bakunin was the prototype of Dostoyevski's Prince Stavrogin in *The Possessed*.[4]

Bakunin took, or made every effort to take, part in all the European uprisings of his time, and even old age and broken health were not enough to stop him, as the incident of Bologna[5] proved. He was twice sentenced to death and was imprisoned for years in the notorious Peter and Paul fortress. After being pardoned and banished to Siberia, he made a romantic escape and, a decade later, reappeared to continue the same work on the same spot, having gone around the world: to Japan, across the Pacific, to America and across the Atlantic Ocean. In later years, when Bakunin staked his hopes on the labor movement of Western Europe, his resultant feud with Marx led to the destruction of the First International.

Tireless activity, whether successful or not, was the passion of Bakunin's life. When, after his escape from Siberia, he came to his friend, Herzen, in London, Bakunin barely stopped to

---

[3] There also is an Italian novel about Bakunin, Ricardo Bacchelli's *The Devil at the Long Bridge*, which has been translated into English.

[4] See *Spor o Bakunine i Dostoyevskom* (Leningrad, 1926).

[5] E. H. Carr, *Michael Bakunin* (London, 1937), pp. 467-469.

exchange greetings before inquiring whether there was unrest in some part of Europe. When Herzen answered that there was not, Bakunin said: "Then what are we to do? Must I go to Persia or India to stir things up? It would drive me mad to sit and do nothing."[6]

On another occasion, Bakunin's friend, Ogarev, reproached him: "You look for bad things to keep yourself busy, without paying any attention to whether this is harmful to the cause."[7] But to Bakunin, this was hardly a reproach. He elevated destruction itself to the rank of a program. In his famous *Confession*, which Bakunin wrote in prison on the order of Tsar Nicholas I, he frankly acknowledged:

> I frequently told the Germans and Poles, when they argued in my presence about future governmental systems: "We are called to destroy, not to build; those who build will be better, wiser and fresher than we."[8]

Richard Wagner, who with Bakunin took part in the Dresden uprising, testified that Bakunin inevitably turned every discussion to the theme of destruction, and that all of Wagner's efforts to elaborate his esthetic aspirations remained unsuccessful.[9] Thus, Bakunin richly deserved the frequently applied epithet of "apostle of pan-destruction."

He was well suited by nature for the role which he chose. It is hardly possible to enumerate all the attributes of Bakunin's personality which facilitated his task. As E. H. Carr says: "The personality of Bakunin is one of those phenomena which cannot be explained in rational terms."[10] Bakunin's colossal stature, his strange style of daily life, his night-long Russian conversation and tea-drinking sessions, even his immense unpaid debts and his queer habits, such as that of often sleeping with his clothes on, all combined to make him a legend even while he was alive. His extraordinary ability to make acquaintances enabled him to move everywhere, among all circles of society. When he arrived in Stockholm on his way to try to take a part in the Polish uprising of 1863, he soon succeeded in being received in a

[6] A. I. Herzen, *Polnoye sobraniye sochinenii i pisem*, M. K. Lemke, ed. (Petrograd, 1919-1923), XV, 12.
[7] M. Dragomanov, *Pisma M. A. Bakunina k A. I. Gerzenu i N. P. Ogarevu* (Geneva, 1896), p. 88.
[8] V. Polonski, *Materialy dlya biografii M. Bakunina* (Moscow-Petrograd, 1923), I, 176-177.
[9] Richard Wagner, *Mein Leben* (Munich, 1911), I, 460ff.
[10] Carr, *op. cit.*, p. 143.

private audience by King Charles XV.[11] Within a short time, Bakunin was "basking in the blaze of Swedish publicity kindled by Baron de Greer's article,"[12] and Christian Hammer, a noted Swedish jeweler and patron of the arts, arranged a banquet in honor of this messenger of revolution and socialism.[13] But on another occasion, when J. Guillaume invited Bakunin to visit the *Fédération Romande,* he won the lasting admiration of the workers of La Locle, Switzerland, with the same ease. After his escape from Siberia, Bakunin made a short, unexpected stop in Boston on his way to London. Even then he was armed with letters of introduction to many outstanding Americans, such as Governor Andrew of Massachusetts, Henry Wilson, the historian who later wrote *Slave Power,* General McClellan, who had been in Russia in 1855-56, Samuel Longfellow, the brother and biographer of Henry Wadsworth Longfellow, and George H. Snelling, a prominent Bostonian and a partisan of the Polish Insurrection of 1831.[14]

Bakunin's aristocratic background and education provided him with the cosmopolitan characteristics of this class. These, in addition to Bakunin's relatively good command of foreign languages, greatly facilitated his acclimatization to the West. Bakunin was one of the few revolutionaries, and of those few perhaps the foremost, whose revolutionary activity was not limited to a single country. Bakunin's activity embraced the whole of eastern Europe, and his participation in and influence on the revolutionary movements of western Europe was no less great. He could rightly say to his faithful friend, N. P. Ogarev, who, like Bakunin, was a political émigré: "You are only Russian, I am an internationalist."[15] Thus, Bakunin stormed, with a giant's stride, through all of Europe of the 19th century. The results of this feverish activity were rather unexpected. His fame and popularity in no wise surpassed his influence. His influence far transcended any measurable achievement which can be credited to him.

In looking for the underlying reason for Bakunin's way of

[11] *Ibid.,* p. 289.
[12] *Ibid.,* p. 291.
[13] Yu. Steklov, *Mikhail Aleksandrovich Bakunin—yego zhizn' i deyatelnost,* II, 224.
[14] D. Hecht, *Russian Radicals Look to America* (Cambridge, 1947), pp. 56-57.
[15] Dragomanov, *op. cit.,* p. 300.

life, for his attitude toward the problems he faced, and for the means which he applied to their solution, it must be conceded that his own temperament was basic. Of course, like everyone else, he was shaped by his epoch, but in his case, external factors played a relatively secondary role. However, his character was so contradictory that Bakunin was an enigma for his contemporaries, as he has been for posterity.

His contemporaries were puzzled by his unbalanced nature. Bakunin's friend, Belinsky, wrote to Botkin: "He [Bakunin] is positively a riddle to me: an abstract hero, born to ruin himself and others, a man with a wonderful head but absolutely without a heart, and with the blood of a stinking salted fish."[16] Herzen judged Bakunin as: "A man of talent, but a scoundrel."[17] On another occasion, he called him "a Columbus without America or even a ship."[18] Pederzolli, who knew Bakunin in Lugano during his last years, described him as "at the same time a child, a savage and a sage."[19]

An extensive citation could be made from such judgments of Bakunin's character by his contemporaries. But the contradictoriness of Bakunin's character influenced not only his relations with his companions and his private life, but also his political action and even his political doctrine. Therefore, it is necessary to understand the contradictions in his character in order to comprehend his political deeds and their ideological rationalizations.

Bakunin's letters, his schemes for conspiratorial organizations, and his whole style of life show that he believed himself predestined to fulfill some extraordinary historical mission. At the age of twenty-six, he wrote from Berlin to his family (November 4, 1842):

> A great future still awaits me. My presentiments cannot deceive me. Oh, if I can only achieve a tiny part of all that is in my heart, I ask nothing more. I do not seek happiness, I do not think of happiness. Deeds, holy arduous deeds, are what I ask. Before me lies a broad field, and my part will be no mean one.[20]

The *leitmotiv* of Bakunin's *Confession*, his account of his

[16] Quoted in Steklov, *op. cit.*, I, 93.
[17] Herzen, *op. cit.*, III, 100.
[18] *Ibid.*, XIII, 573.
[19] Quoted in Steklov, *op. cit.*, IV, 392.
[20] Bakunin, *Works*, Steklov ed., III, 151.

revolutionary activity up to 1849, was that he considered himself better fitted than any other to turn the course of the March Revolution along the right way. His conviction of his irrevocable mission did not diminish in his later years, and in all his schemes for conspiratorial organizations he provided a crucial position for himself.

At the same time, he showed an almost complete disregard for his own fame and glory. It was not a desire for personal vainglory which provided the stimulus for his deeds and for the role which he laid out for himself. Therefore, he was always ready to offer the position of apparent leadership to someone else (at one time even to Governor-general Muraviev-Amurski). But he always reserved the real management of his revolution for himself. In a letter to Albert Richard, he wrote:

> You tell me that I can become the Garibaldi of socialism. I have very little desire to become a Garibaldi and play a grotesque role. My dear sir, I shall die and the worms will eat me, but I want our idea to triumph. I want the masses of humanity to be truly emancipated from all authorities and from all heroes present and to come.

In another passage of the same letter we read:

> Do you know the limits of my entire ambition? My ambition is great, but it does not lead to a noisy fame; it is this, to help you to build that invisible collective power [i.e. secret revolutionary society] which alone can lead and save the revolution.[21]

This unusual mixture of conviction of the greatness of his mission with a lack of desire for personal glory made his erratic leadership tolerable; sometimes he was even followed blindly. The absence of selfishness in Bakunin was a great attraction to his followers; perhaps it even served as a substitute for any real achievements.

It was also characteristic of Bakunin's temperament that he always strove for the real direction of an undertaking in which he participated. He could not tolerate any real rivals. This compulsion to exercise uncontested leadership led Bakunin into many conflicts with his friends, followers, and opponents. However, he always preferred to be the commander-in-chief in his own society, in which the rank and file sometimes scarcely existed

[21] Polonski, *Materialy*, III, 258ff.

outside his own imagination, than to take part in great movements in which he might expect to play an important, but not
the only leading, role. This attitude was certainly related to
Bakunin's conviction of his extraordinary historical mission.

On the other hand, when Bakunin met an unusually energetic
personality, he succumbed readily. We see this in his relationship with Governor-general Muraviev or with Nechaev. In the
latter case, the legendary revolutionary veteran submitted to the
command of a twenty-one year old adventurer who, though he
had the ambitions of a field marshal was still a raw recruit.

The magic of Bakunin's personality bewitched his circle of
acquaintances, and these were indeed a motley company.
Vyrubov, a Russian émigré who knew Bakunin in Naples, wrote
somewhat sarcastically:

> With open arms Bakunin welcomed youngsters, adults
> and old people, the wise and the fools, the learned and
> the ignorant, the citizens of all countries, those of all pro-
> fessions and convictions—if only they would listen to his
> revolutionary preaching, which indeed he was able to
> conduct masterfully and in a number of languages.[22]

Bakunin had few rivals in his ability to compel the admiration
and confidence of new acquaintances. He infatuated others at
first sight. As Herzen wrote: "There was something childlike,
kindly and simple in him; this gave him an unusual charm and
attracted to him both the strong and the weak."[23] He was able
to become the center of attention quickly, but his influence was
seldom of long duration. He parted from almost all with whom
he came into contact, and these farewells were frequently stormy
and sometimes decidedly dramatic. Only when the basis of
friendship was completely apolitical, as in the case of the
musician, Alfred Reichel, were the friendships lasting.

Bakunin became infatuated himself as easily as he infatuated
others. It is hardly possible to describe all the conceptions,
ideologies, ideas, and plans which he seized upon from every
corner of the social horizon, and which met, stimulated each
other, and amalgamated or clashed within Bakunin's mind. The
curious composite of his thought and action is becoming clear
only now, with the perspective of almost a century.

Another facet of Bakunin's personality must be understood,

[22] *Vestnik Evropy* (February, 1913), p. 79.
[23] Herzen, *op. cit.*, XIV, 429.

his extraordinary political foresight. He was able to perceive, analyze, and predict the course of social and political processes which at the time were in an embryonic state. As early as 1843, before Bakunin had met Marx, Engels, and Proudhon, he declared in an article in *Der Schweizerische Republikaner* that communism was a world problem. In the same article, he criticized the lack, in communist doctrine, of a program for solving the national question.[24]

In his *Appeal to the Slavs*, published in the fall of 1848, he clearly and correctly defined two of the main issues of the future when he stated that:

> Two great questions have come to the fore since early this spring: the social question and that of the independence of all nations: the emancipation of the peoples both internally and externally. It was not a few individuals, it was not a party, it was the unerring instinct of the masses which has elevated these two questions above all others and demanded their prompt solution.[25]

Bakunin's premonition of the rebirth of the "non-historical" nations induced him to demand self-determination for nations which, in his time, were rather in the condition of ethnic protoplasm. For this reason, he advocated, as a primary task, the breaking up of the multinational Hapsburg and Russian Empires. E. H. Carr makes the following comment on the *Appeal to the Slavs:*

> For this, if for no other, reason the *Appeal to the Slavs* is a landmark in European history. It was the first occasion on which, exactly seventy years before November 1918, the destruction of the Austrian Empire and the building up of new Slav states were publicly advocated.[26]

One of the main themes of Bakunin's *Statism and Anarchy* was that the strivings of the Germans for unity endangered their democracy. Even some of his very occasional remarks on the United States are not lacking in farsightedness.[27]

However, Bakunin combined this clairvoyance with an almost unlimited naïveté, particularly when he was occupied with the problem of revolution. Then skepticism had no place in his

[24] Bakunin, *Works,* Steklov ed., III, 227ff.
[25] J. Pfitzner, *Bakuninstudien* (Prague, 1932), p. 101.
[26] Carr, *op. cit.,* p. 175.
[27] Cf. Hecht, *op. cit.,* Chapter IV.

mind. Thus, Bakunin vastly overestimated the potentialities of every uprising which took place in the Europe of his day. His predictions about the course of these uprisings were seldom fulfilled. He usually managed to see the germ of world revolution and of the downfall of the old order in the least unrest. And if his plans of action were sometimes theoretically correct (as was perhaps the case when he advocated the alliance of the German democrats and the Slavs to fight absolutism during the March Revolution), the preconditions necessary for the realization of his proposals usually did not exist. Therefore, these projects were illusory. The same holds true of the secret societies and revolutionary organizations which he spent his life trying to build up; he was simply unable to estimate their true strength.

In such situations, Bakunin sometimes resorted to mystification. It is not easy to say whether or not Bakunin was aware of what he was doing. It was his boundless imagination which inspired Bakunin to propose the placing of the Sistine Madonna on the city walls of Dresden when the Prussian troops were approaching the rebellious city, in the hope that this would deter them from bombarding it.[28] The same boundless imagination led him to think of offering the leadership of his revolution to Muraviev, or even to the tsar, or to consider Italian free masonry a fitting tool for his revolutionary plans. He certainly did not lack audacity. In a speech at a banquet in his honor in Stockholm, in 1863, Bakunin described the small, weak Russian secret society, *Land and Freedom*, as a "vast association which is at the same time patriotic, conservative, liberal, and democratic." According to him, it counted among its members "all the classes of Russians of good-will, whatever their rank or position: generals and officers *en masse*, major and minor officials, aristocratic landowners, merchants, priests and sons of priests, peasants, and millions of the dissenters."[29] This, however, was nothing but a barefaced lie.

Parallel to his own talent for mystification was his inability to see through the abracadabra of others. He often was a victim of make-believe. Perhaps the most curious example is that of Nechaev, who presented himself as the chief of a huge Russian underground organization, and easily hoodwinked Bakunin.

[28] Herzen, *op. cit.*, XIV, 425.
[29] Dragomanov, *op. cit.*, p. 142.

This strange mixture of clearsightedness and naïveté was a basic source of Bakunin's confusion. The clear judgment displayed in many of his utterances saved him from being considered as a mere maniac. But his wishful thinking and frequent escapes into the realm of imagination and mystification resulted in his losing his grasp of reality and his standard of judgment for the achievements of himself or of others.

Bakunin's deeds, which he so vaunted, were scarcely more clear cut. As we have seen, Bakunin considered vigorous, effective action as his primary, or even his exclusive, task. In a letter to Emma Herwegh (February, 1843), he wrote: "In my opinion quiet, which everyone rates so highly, is the greatest disaster which can befall a human being."[30] He often repeated that enough programs had already been produced and that what was needed was their realization. Thus, he harnessed his titanic energy and overwhelming vitality to action, but the results eluded him. He used bravado and his innate cunning as props, but they were of little avail. Therefore, he switched from one operation to another with such rapidity that he seldom finished what he had begun. He did not even scorn trickery and theatrical extravaganza. In his secret societies, strange oaths were sworn on daggers and pistols, and needless ciphers were used plentifully. All this did not save Bakunin's projects from misfire, or himself from much personal disappointment. Thomas Masaryk writes:

> If the anarchists esteem Bakunin as a man of action, they are mistaken; he was a dilettante of action. His practical, like his theoretical, life, was a patchwork of fragments.[31]

There was another ambiguity and contradiction in Bakunin's character, one which was perhaps the most curious and not without consequence. In spite of Bakunin's immense fanaticism, he was by no means an ascetic. His fanaticism is proved by his whole career, and he consciously cultivated it. His lifelong friend, the musician, Reichel, testifies that although Bakunin was very fond of listening to the music of Beethoven, he reproached himself for this as a weakness which took him away from his task of revolution.[32] In a letter to his brother, Paul, and to

[30] Bakunin, *Works,* Steklov ed., III, 179.
[31] T. G. Masaryk, *Russland und Europa* (Jena, 1913), II, 34.
[32] *Spor o Bakunine i Dostoyevskom,* pp. 36-37.

Turgenev, he wrote: "I only know that I shall not slacken speed as long as there is a drop of blood left in me."[33] He rephrased this to Ogarev (June 14, 1868) in the following way: "I shall continue to be an impossible person as long as those who are now possible remain possible."[34] However, strange as it may seem, Bakunin did not demonstrate the slightest tendency toward asceticism. His humor, his incomparable nonchalance, his social manners of a negligent Russian *grand seigneur,* and his taste for eating well, drinking enough, and smoking incessantly, kept him from seeming like a professional revolutionary, and made him appear more like a Bohemian. Bakunin's strange mixture of fanaticism and sybaritism is manifest at every step. He himself best described it when he gave the following amusing definition of the seven degrees of human happiness to the workers of La Locle: 1) death fighting for liberty, 2) love and friendship, 3) the arts and sciences, 4) smoking, 5) drinking, 6) eating, and 7) sleeping.[35]

The result of this strange amalgam was that although Bakunin preached a dire program of destruction and tried to put it into practice, in his mouth his words sometimes lost their dire accents. They often became harmless, sometimes even droll. Many of those around him perceived this. Berdyaev called Bakunin "in his personality and style of life an all too fantastic representative of the Russian *Barstvo* [nobility]. To the end of his days, he remained a great child enchanted with the most radical revolutionary ideas, a Russian fantastic, incapable of methodical thought, a Stenka Razin of the Russian nobility."[36]

But when Bakunin's fanaticism and abilities were crossed with the amorality and obsessions of others, then things took another turn. Then there were mad moments of causeless brutality. Once again the Nechaev affair provides the most striking example. Bakunin's activity took queer, intolerable forms and gave birth to the *Catechism of the Revolutionary.* From this unsurpassed specimen of revolutionary super-Machiavellianism we select:

> The revolutionist is a doomed man. Everything in
> him is absorbed by one exclusive interest, one thought,

[33] Bakunin, *Works,* Steklov ed., III, 164.   [34] Dragomanov, *op. cit.,* p. 216.
[35] Carr, *op. cit.,* p. 356.
[36] N. Berdiajev, *Sinn und Schicksal des russischen Kommunismus* (Lucerne, 1937), p. 73.

one passion—the revolution. [Art. 1] Day and night he must have one thought, one aim—merciless destruction. [Art. 6] He knows only one science, the science of destruction. [Art. 3] He despises and hates the present day code of morals with all its motivations and manifestations. To him whatever aids the triumph of revolution is ethical; all that which hinders it is unethical and criminal. [Art. 4] Therefore, in getting closer to the people, we must first of all join those elements of the masses which, since the foundation of the Moscow State power, have never ceased to protest, not in words alone but in deed as well, against everything which is directly or indirectly connected with the state. . . . Let us join hands with the bold world of brigands—the only genuine revolutionists in Russia.[37]

In the *Principles of Revolution,* which also stems from the Nechaev period in Bakunin's life, the revolutionary way was described thus:

We recognize no other activity but the work of extermination, but we admit that the forms in which this activity is manifested will be extremely varied—poison, the knife, the rope, etc. In this struggle revolution sanctifies everything equally.[38]

However, when Bakunin's connections with such persons were severed, he was sometimes able to denounce this "Jesuitry," as he called it, and to warn others against applying it.[39] It is difficult to say to what extent such recantations were sincere or to what extent they were merely the result of a temporary vacillation. In any case, they hardly fit with the basic premises of his doctrine.

Thus, Bakunin's psyche was composed of such contradictory and paradoxical elements. Yet his character was the basis of all that Bakunin did. Therefore, it is no wonder that Bakunin's life, as embodied in his deeds and writings, is no less paradoxical. His temperament induced him to be at the same time a commander-in-chief and a common soldier, a political thinker and an executor of ideological programs.

For these reasons, he was as much a riddle for his con-

---

[37] An English translation of the *Catechism of the Revolutionary* is to be found in Max Nomad's *Apostles of Revolution* (Boston, 1939), pp. 228ff.
[38] Dragomanov, *op. cit.,* p. 482.
[39] Such an instance is described in Debogori-Mokriyevich, *Vospominaniya* (St. Petersburg, 1905), pp. 206 ff.; see also Bakunin's letters in Dragomanov, *op. cit.,* pp. 287, 351.

temporaries as he has become an object of controversy for posterity. Of course no political thinker, no political doer, has appeared the same to all of posterity. But in Bakunin's case, it was inevitable that the divergency of opinion about him, his role, and his achievements should have been as wide as is conceivable.

In the opinion of the broad public, which neither can nor wishes to see more clearly, Bakunin has been the embodiment of a mania for the causeless destruction of the existing social order.

For his faithful followers and admirers, who in the course of time have diminished to a small sect, he has become everything. The need of such a small sect to be self-sufficient, which is perhaps the first precondition for its existence, led its members to regard Bakunin not only as the founder of anarchist doctrine and the anarchist movement, but also as a thinker who solved the most crucial philosophical problems of existence. They defended him obstinately against any attack, and refused to acknowledge, or passed over in silence, Bakunin's authorship of those writings which they felt compromised their teacher, even though his authorship is unquestioned today.[40]

To authors who are indifferent to Bakunin's ideological concepts, the curious and sometimes even the comical aspects of his life are the most attractive.[41]

The views of scholars who have made critical studies of Bakunin's role are very divergent. Masaryk says: "Bakunin did not make any essential contribution to the theoretical formulation of either socialism or anarchism; however, his practical example was suggestive not only to practitioners but also to the theoreticians."[42] Polonski, a careful student of Bakunin's life (though not of his doctrine), says: "Despite the splendor and aureola by which this name is surrounded, to call Bakunin a 'theoretician' of anarchism would be an exaggeration."[43] Karl Diehl says that although Bakunin had a great influence on political anarchism, at the same time he did not add anything essential to previous

---

[40] See M. Nettlau's publications about Bakunin; Peter Kropotkin's writings; V. Cherkesov's commentaries; also the recent K. J. Kenafick, *Michael Bakunin and Karl Marx* (Melbourne, 1948); and G. P. Maximoff, *The Political Philosophy of Bakunin—Scientific Anarchism* (Glencoe, 1953).
[41] Cf. the biography of Bakunin best known in the West, that of E. H. Carr.
[42] Masaryk, *op. cit.*, II, 35.
[43] V. Polonski, *Mikhail Aleksandrovich Bakunin* (Moscow, 1920), p. 5.

anarchist theory.[44] Steklov, the chief and official Soviet biographer of Bakunin, author of the four-volume biography and editor-in-chief of the contemplated complete edition of Bakunin's writings, states that Bakunin was the creator of anarchist doctrine which, although compiled from elements taken from others, presents in its entirety a distinctive entity. However, according to Steklov, Bakunin's strength lay "not in theoretical premises and conclusions, and not even so much in organizational work, but primarily in revolutionary agitation."[45]

However, all the authors who were attracted by Bakunin's unusual personality agree on one point: his phenomenal historical significance. Let us limit our quotations to this effect to two authors, one a representative of the West, E. H. Carr, and one a representative of his native country, Steklov.

> Bakunin is one of the completest embodiments in history of the spirit of liberty—the liberty which excludes neither licence nor caprice, which tolerates no human institution, which remains an unrealized and unrealizable ideal, but which is almost universally felt to be an indispensable part of the highest manifestations and aspirations of humanity.[46]

> Bakunin is one of the few Russian political activists who played a global role, and is unquestionably an international figure; but at the same time his is a completely national figure, with all the accessory advantages and disadvantages of personal and social singularities. Bakunin was the founder not only of European anarchism, but also of Russian populist rebellionism, and therefore of Russian Social Democracy, from which the Communist Party emerged.[47]

---

[44] Karl Diehl, *Ueber Sozialismus, Kommunismus und Anarchismus* (Jena, 1911), pp. 124, 125.

[45] Steklov, *op. cit.*, III, 131 ff., and I, 263.

[46] Carr, *op. cit.*, p. 440.

[47] Steklov, *op. cit.*, I, 9.

CHAPTER 2

BAKUNIN AS A POLITICAL THINKER

ALTHOUGH Bakunin's position as one of the founders of the modern anarchist movement cannot be challenged, the opinions cited at the end of the previous chapter are enough to show that there is a general tendency to deny that Bakunin played an essential role in the formulation of anarchist doctrine. This is the prevailing view,[1] and it is repudiated only by Bakunin's devoted followers and admirers.[2]

To give a provisional estimate of Bakunin's political doctrine (the whole essay should provide a detailed one), there seems to be good reason for considering Bakunin as the creator of an anarchist doctrine which, whether it is realizable or utopian, does provide a critique of the existing order, a rather vague outline of a future social order, and a relatively detailed program for achieving this. It is true that this doctrine was composed of elements borrowed from other thinkers, but this is the case with many doctrines. Bakunin gives these borrowed theorems a substantially different meaning and creates an organic and distinct entity. Therefore, it seems that the general opinion, which denies that Bakunin made a basic formulation of anarchist doctrine, is inadequate.

However, there are readily apparent reasons for the prevailing opinion that Bakunin did not make any intrinsic contribution to anarchist doctrine. Perhaps the first is Bakunin's own evaluation of the worth of his theoretical contribution, and of the role of theory in general.

In a letter of May 7, 1872, to A. Lorenzo, a Spanish internationalist, Bakunin wrote:

---

[1] Cf. Masaryk, *op. cit.*, II, 35; Polonski, *M. A. Bakunin,* p. 5; A. Gray, *The Socialist Tradition* (London-New York, 1947), p. 353; G. Catlin, *The Story of the Political Philosophers* (New York, 1939), p. 427; K. Diehl, *Ueber Socialismus . . .*, p. 125; and in part Steklov, *op. cit.*, I, 263.

[2] P. Kropotkin, M. Nettlau, G. P. Maximoff, K. J. Kenafick, V. Cherkesov.

You know, citizen, that whenever it pleases them, they
[Marx's followers] depict me as the head of a school of the
"International" which they call anarchist. This is an honor
and dishonor which I do not deserve under any circumstances. I am not a philosopher, and not a creator of
systems like Marx.[3]

In another letter to Lorenzo (May 10, 1872), Bakunin
restated this:

I declare once and for all that, just as I never invented
any system, nor even what might be called one new idea,
I do not have the right to be called a ringleader or chief in
any theoretical meaning of these words.[4]

It is true that on another occasion Bakunin wrote: "I, who
have worked so much in theory, who have shown myself to be
a jealous guardian of revolutionary principles . . ."[5] Indeed, this
is perhaps a truer expression of Bakunin's real inner conviction
about his role as a theoretician, but the view which gained
currency was that he renounced any ambition to be considered
as a political ideologist.

Such an opinion is compatible with Bakunin's attitude toward
the role of theory in general, which was on the whole a
nihilistic one. In an article of 1869 printed in *Narodnaya
Rosprava,* No. 1, which was published by Bakunin and Nechaev,[6]
we find the following statement: "We frankly refuse to work out
projects for future conditions. This is not within the scope of
our activity, since we consider mere theoretical reasoning use-
less."[7] In a letter (January 23, 1873) to S. Ralli, a Russian émigré
who at one time was his collaborator, Bakunin wrote: "Life, my
dear friend, is always broader than doctrine; life is not to be
squeezed into the framework of any doctrine, not even one as
all-embracing as our anarchism."[8]

Bakunin once called Marx's *Capital* a "dreadful book of 784
pages of small print."[9] At another time he termed it "economic

---

[3] Steklov, *op. cit.,* III, 112.   [4] *Ibid.,* pp. 115-116.
[5] Bakunin, *Works, Golos Truda* edition, II, 176.
[6] The authorship of this article has been disputed. Steklov advances convincing arguments in favor of the thesis that Bakunin wrote it. (Cf.
Steklov's *M. A. Bakunin,* III, 433-457.) However, this question is of
secondary importance since Nechaev was so much Bakunin's inferior
intellectually that he was compelled to borrow his ideological concepts
from the latter.
[7] Quoted in Steklov, *op. cit.,* III, 455.
[8] *O minuvshem,* Historical Almanac (St. Petersburg, 1909), pp. 333-334.
[9] Dragomanov, *op. cit.,* p. 247.

metaphysics."[10] Bakunin's attitude toward theory appeared more conciliatory when he said that the task of elaborating theoretical systems should be left to others: "Let us leave to others the task of developing the theoretical principles of social revolution and content ourselves with applying them, with incorporating them into acts."[11] But, in general, his attitude toward theory may be summed up in his own words: "I cleave to no system, I am a true seeker."[12] "I am neither a scholar nor a philosopher, nor even a writer, by vocation."[13]

Another source of confusion about Bakunin's position as a theoretician arose from the role which he allotted to revolution. It would logically appear that revolution should only be a means for achieving a new political or social order. But Bakunin's scheme was rather different. He believed that the destruction of the existing order needed to be so complete that it would require all the attention and efforts of at least one generation. The task of building a new order should, therefore, be left to posterity.

Even before the March Revolution, Bakunin had defined revolution as follows: "But revolution is instinct rather than thought, it operates as an instinct, and as an instinct it gives first battle."[14] Such an approach left little room for theoretical elaborations and considerations. What was left? Perhaps only questions of revolutionary strategy and tactics. Bakunin's view did not change in his later life; it was only that his language became less ceremonious. In his *Principles of Revolution,* which dates from the period of his collaboration with Nechaev, we read:

> The dilettantes and Philistines of science, the satiated speculators of the good old days, in their fight against the idea of general revolution always wrote long dissertations on the same theme: "Without a closely elaborated program for construction, one dare not destroy. . . ." We say, "Total destruction is incompatible with plans for construction." It must start with a genuine revolution, with a complete transformation of all of the conditions of social life. The present generation must destroy blindly, indiscriminately, everything that exists, thinking only "as fast

[10] *Ibid.,* p. 252.
[11] Bakunin, *Works, Golos Truda* ed., IV, 176.
[12] Quoted in Carr, *op. cit.,* p. 167.
[13] Bakunin, *Gesammelte Werke,* II, 268.
[14] Bakunin, *Works,* Steklov ed., III, 317.

as possible, as much as possible"; and because the present generation grew up under the influence of those abominable conditions, it shall not be allowed the task of construction.[15]

Thus, revolution itself is made a self-sufficient aim. Albert Camus paraphrases Bakunin's own words to say that revolution shall be: ". . . 'A feast without beginning and without end.' In fact for him [Bakunin], as for all who are oppressed, the revolution is a feast in the religious sense of this word."[16]

After such a projected total revolution, which is equated to social catastrophe and total destruction, any program for the future social order is considered superfluous. Bakunin is consistent in stating that:

> For those who have already committed themselves to the cause of revolution, all talk about the distant future is criminal, since it distracts from pure destruction and stems the tide of revolution.[17]

In addition to these handicaps to Bakunin as a political thinker, we find that he was not even a truly theoretical writer. This is shown by the very form of Bakunin's writings. He was not, as he himself acknowledged,[18] a writer by vocation, even though he frequently took pen in hand, usually for immediate propaganda purposes. Then he wrote eloquently, brilliantly, and often convincingly. However, his proper element was always agitation, debate, public speaking, and conspiracy. Among his extensive and feverish activities, writing was only an auxiliary. As his activity slowed down, his writing also came to a stop. Thus, during the last years of his life, which were comparatively quiet, his literary production almost ceased. He always started to write under the pressure of a given occasion, and discontinued his efforts when the pressure was lifted. He never returned to old material. Thus, his writings are a disconnected series of fragmentary articles, essays, and pamphlets, most of them unfinished, almost all of them poorly composed. The main theme is usually lost among extremely long digressions, which break the whole into fragments, without rising to the level of entities in themselves.

Bakunin was a diligent letter writer, and many of his letters

[15] Dragomanov, *op. cit.*, pp. 479-480.
[16] Albert Camus, *The Rebel* (New York, 1954), p. 129.
[17] Dragomanov, *op. cit.*, p. 480.
[18] Bakunin, *Gesammelte Werke*, II, 268; III, 160.

afford a key to his writings and his thoughts. They are of no little importance toward the understanding of him and his teachings. Taken all together, Bakunin's literary output was considerable.[19]

In Bakunin's writings, we find deficiencies not only in form but also in content. Nearly all contain inconsistencies, obscurities, and striking contradictions. Thematically, they may be divided into two groups, one concerned with daily political issues, the other expounding philosophical themes. All are polemical and most of them aggressive. Some seem to have been written in the grip of an obsession. Bakunin's philosophical digressions cover almost all conceivable problems, and in them he does not seem to have had the gift of clarity. Here Bakunin's resemblance to the French utopian thinkers, by whom he was influenced, is noticeable. Although in these philosophical reasonings we find some accurate and pertinent statements (in regard to one, Catlin remarks, perhaps too precipitately, that if Bakunin "had written nothing other than these words, for their wisdom alone the great Anarchist would deserve a place in history."[20]), they are all perverted by the fact that most of Bakunin's philosophical pronouncements were evoked by non-philosophical causes. He used philosophy in an arbitrary manner for the support of his socio-political premises. These, however, were not usually reached by the means of philosophical cognition. The philosophical superstructure was imposed on top of ready-made ideological and political conclusions. In the revolutionary era of his life, Bakunin's attitude toward philosophy was, on the whole, a utilitarian one, and therefore his extensive variations on philosophical themes contribute little toward an understanding of his political doctrine.

Nowhere do we find a consecutive exposition of Bakunin's views as a whole. Instead, we have a series of isolated pronouncements on the problem of anarchism scattered throughout Bakunin's essays, pamphlets, and articles, as well as in his letters and in the statutes of his secret societies. The only way to reconstruct Bakunin's political doctrine of anarchism is to dis-

[19] The projected complete Soviet edition of Bakunin's works was to have been made up of twelve volumes of about 300 pages each (see Steklov, *op. cit.*, I, 11). This project was never completed. The four volumes which did appear contained Bakunin's works up to 1861, i.e. up to the time of his escape from Siberia. All of the other editions of Bakunin's works are incomplete, and also deficient for many other reasons.

[20] Catlin, *op. cit.*, p. 430.

entangle these statements from the jungle of his reasoning. However, this is not all that has to be done. As E. H. Carr remarks:

> Bakunin suffered the fate of those whose influence on their contemporaries depends on the spoken word and on that elusive gift called personality. It was impossible to convey to posterity that sense of overwhelming power which was always present to those who knew him in his life.[21]

In other words, the example of his own life was part of Bakunin's doctrine. Therefore, a penetrating study of all the expressions of Bakunin's life and an accurate interpretation of the symptoms of his spiritual functioning help substantially in overcoming the difficulties met in dealing with his doctrine. Any exposition of Bakunin's ideology which draws only upon his political writings in a strict sense cannot be exact.[22] His life must also be taken into account. It is no accident that Bakunin's writings have never been re-edited in any appreciable quantity, and that biography rather than critical analysis has been the chief manner of treatment. There are many biographies, some of them very extensive.[23] And they continue to appear. These biographies are, however, only a partial substitute for an evaluation of his doctrine. On the whole they are unsuccessful and sometimes even distort Bakunin's doctrine.

We have seen Bakunin's deficiencies as a political writer. Do they negate his right to be called a political thinker? Certainly they make it difficult to measure his theoretical contribution by the normal standards. However, they hardly deprive him of the right to be considered as, if not a political philosopher in a strict sense of this word, at least an outstanding exponent of political theory.

---

[21] Carr, *op. cit.*, p. 439.

[22] An obvious example of such an unsuccessful experience is the selection of Bakunin's writings entitled *The Political Philosophy of Bakunin: Scientific Anarchism*, compiled by G. P. Maximoff (Glencoe, Free Press, 1953), to be cited as Maximoff. This is the more true since Maximoff eliminated all of Bakunin's writings which orthodox anarchists consider as compromising to their leader, although Bakunin's authorship is unquestionable today. Maximoff disregarded, for instance, the statutes of Bakunin's secret societies and his famous Catechisms.

[23] Steklov's four volumes total 2058 pages, V. Polonski's three-volume *Materialy dlya biografii Bakunina* has 1744 pages, Kornilov's biography of Bakunin's youth is in two volumes of 1302 pages.

CHAPTER 3

THE GENEALOGY OF BAKUNIN'S THOUGHT

THE CONTRADICTIONS of Bakunin's character could not fail to leave their imprint on his political doctrine. His doctrine is a strange amalgam of alien, borrowed ideas and theorems, seldom completely digested or explained, and in addition given a sloppy literary presentation. Therefore, an exposition of Bakunin's doctrine has always been preceded by the question of whether all the elements of Bakunin's thoughts form a totality. This has been answered in various ways.

A presentation of the genealogy of Bakunin's thought might be of great help toward a correct and final comprehension of his doctrine of anarchism. This, however, would require a complete study in itself, and perhaps it would still be impossible to unravel some of the entanglements. On this point, it should never be forgotten that Bakunin was primarily a political man of action, and that therefore he had sometimes to abstain from expressing his ideas fully, for tactical reasons. There is little doubt that more than once Bakunin softened the expression of his views if he felt that they were too radical to be acceptable to the audience addressed. However, it is hardly possible to give a general rule for the determination of when this is the case.

This chapter can only be a sketch of the genealogy of Bakunin's thought, giving some hints and indications, but abstaining from any final conclusions or evaluation.

Ideologically, Bakunin's life may be divided into two major periods.[1] The first covers his stay in his native country, with

[1] There was still another short period in Bakunin's life, that of his last two years, when his lifelong revolutionary optimism flagged. This was primarily caused by Bakunin's discovery that the revolutionary instinct which he had always credited to the masses was lacking, and did not really affect his belief in the idea and expediency of revolution as such. In a letter to Elisée Reclus, he stated: "To my utter despair I have discovered, and discover every day anew, that there is in the masses no revolutionary idea or hope or passion." (Bakunin, *Gesammelte Werke*, III, 272.) From

21

a rather short extension abroad, during Bakunin's zealous attempt to study philosophy; the second embraces his revolutionary activity, including the decade of his imprisonment and banishment. This second period had two stages: during the first, his revolutionary zeal was dedicated to revolutionary Pan-Slavism; during the second, to anarchism. Bakunin's feverish revolutionary activity and his concept of revolution form the connecting links between the Pan-Slavic and the anarchist periods. During the March Revolution of 1848, Bakunin's scheme of revolution was already established, and from then on he did not make any substantial revisions in it. The anarchist doctrine was simply adapted to this concept of revolution.

Indeed, there is no real gap between his philosophical and revolutionary periods. This was due to Bakunin's personal attitude toward philosophy, which he regarded as a means for the complete reconstruction of the social environment. Therefore, although an ideological graph of Bakunin's life would show precipitous ups and downs, there is also something essentially homogeneous in his life. This comes from the fact that he was always an extremist in his attitude toward everything. This intensity acts as a common denominator for all the stages of his life and for everything which he did.

Bakunin became acquainted with philosophy early. Although he owed his first push in this direction to an accident (as an artillery officer he fortuitously obtained a small pamphlet by Venevitinov: *Philosophical Letters to the Countess N. H.*[2]), his whole enthusiasm for philosophy proceeded along the usual path of contemporary Russian intellectuals. The 1840s were years of cultural stimulation in Russia. German idealistic philosophy was the main interest of this generation, and curiosity about this philosophy spread with the speed of an epidemic.[3] Moscow, the old capital, was the center of these aspirations; the famous "circles" were the very embodiment of these strivings. These circles were all connected with the University. In the early thirties a remarkable group of undergraduates at the University of Moscow formed two circles, that of Stankevich and that of Herzen. The former was devoted to an enthusiastic study of

the doctrinal point of view, this period of Bakunin's life is not of particular importance, since it did not force him to ideological revisionism.

[2] B. P. Hepner, *Bakounine et le panslavisme révolutionnaire* (Paris, 1950), p. 56.

[3] Chizhevski, *op. cit.*, p. 33.

idealistic philosophy: Schelling, Fichte, Hegel. Herzen's circle concentrated on political and social questions, and the members were the first in Russia to propagate the doctrines of Saint-Simon and Fourier. The University of Moscow was a crucible in which all classes were fused into a non-class intelligentsia.

Bakunin's quest took him to Stankevich's circle, and, after the latter went abroad, Bakunin quickly succeeded in becoming the philosophical authority of this group. The atmosphere of this circle has been called "enthusiastic, eschatological, fantastic, romantic."[4] Bakunin found himself in his own element. As D. I. Chizhevski says: "In the whole history of Russian thought there is no other example equal in force to Bakunin's philosophical fanaticism."[5] The whole of Bakunin's temperament at once found an opportunity for expression. However, Bakunin was not satisfied with his position as philosophical authority, and strove to become the uncontested dictator of the circle. He sought either submissive followers or foes. All of reality was questioned and considered problematic, as demanding justification. Even at this time, Bakunin felt the need to carry on propaganda, which he did by way of preaching sermons. His letters to his family and friends turned into long dissertations and exalted manifestoes.

Bakunin intended to study the philosophy of Kant, Schelling, and Fichte. However, it appears that he did not study Schelling, and Kant only very superficially. He concentrated on Fichte.[6] He read Fichte's *Guide to a Blessed Life*, and translated his lectures, *On the Vocation of the Scholar*, into Russian. Bakunin united his interest in Fichte with one in German romantic poetry. He was enraptured by Schiller, Jean Paul, Hoffman, and Bettina von Arnim. Under this combined influence of literary romanticism and Fichte's dialectical mysticism, with its basis in a dualistic concept of the world, Bakunin developed a unique blend of youthful rebelliousness in which love was combined with hate, liberty with intolerance.[7] A. A. Kornilov, the noted Russian historian and biographer of young Bakunin, draws the surprising conclusion that the logical consequence of Bakunin's ideas while he was under the influence of Fichte would have been a Christian anarchism analogous to that of Tolstoy.[8] From Fichte, Bakunin learned that "the aim of life" is "God," but not the God

---

[4] *Ibid.*, p. 55.
[5] *Ibid.*, p. 84.
[6] *Ibid.*, p. 88.
[7] Hepner, *op. cit.*, p. 80.
[8] A. A. Kornilov, *Molodye Gody M. Bakunina* (Moscow, 1915), p. 232.

to whom prayers are said in churches, rather a God who lives in mankind and who ascends with the ascension of mankind.[9] At that time, he made a firm pronouncement that: "There is no God in slavery, God exists only in freedom."[10]

Bakunin's exaltation of Fichte did not, however, last very long. Early in 1837 Bakunin proceeded to the study of Hegel. He worked very hard. After digesting a text of logic, he moved to the works of Hegel himself, beginning with the *Phenomenology of the Spirit,* but soon abandoning this in favor of the *Encyclopedia.* Here, in the introduction, Bakunin first encountered that famous dictum which impressed him so extremely, and which was to become the platform for lively controversy among the members of the above-mentioned circles: "That which is rational is real, and that which is real is rational." He moved also to the *Philosophy of Religion,* and later returned to the *Phenomenology.* The task of mastering Hegel's philosophy, which Bakunin, who had had no systematic philosophic training, imposed upon himself was certainly a difficult one.[11]

Carr says: "He [Bakunin] never achieved any thorough mastery of the Hegelian system."[12] Chizhevski, an acknowledged authority on philosophy in eastern Europe, and especially on the influence of Hegel's philosophy on Russian thought, states that: "Bakunin's knowledge of Hegel was thorough and serious."[13] Weight is given to Chizhevski's opinion by the fact that when Bakunin was later in Germany, he was able to play an important role among the leading German left Hegelians.

The transition from Fichte to Hegel brought little change in Bakunin's phraseology.[14] In fact, the shift to Hegel intensified his rapture over philosophy. It may be said that for him Hegel's philosophy became a sort of new religion. Thus, Bakunin even applied his philosophical schemes to the solution of his personal problems. We meet typical mystical conceptions of catharsis through union with God. In a letter (February 11, 1837) of that period, he writes: "This unity of human beings with God is what establishes the divine external world." At the same time, however, we hear a note which is more innate to Bakunin; we are

---

[9] Chizhevski, *op. cit.,* p. 88.
[10] Kornilov, *Molodye Gody,* p. 194. Two decades later Bakunin's device was just the opposite. Then he vigorously supported the thesis: "If God exists, man is a slave, but man can and must be free, therefore God does not exist."
[11] Carr, *op. cit.,* p. 60.
[12] *Ibid.,* p. 61.
[13] *Chizhevski, op. cit.,* p. 98.
[14] *Ibid.,* p. 107.

told that the way to establish this "new external world" is at the same time the way of destruction. "Harmony will be destroyed by contact with the world because, as Hegel says, harmony which originates from the home [i.e., on the basis of traditional upbringing] is not true harmony,"[15] writes Bakunin in a letter of February 20, 1837.

In the preface to his translation of Hegel's *Gymnasialreden* (printed in *Nabludatel,* Moscow, 1838), Bakunin condemns all of French 18th century philosophy, and also Saint-Simonism, because of its atheism, and affirms that "Frenchmen do not know, and do not want to know, Christianity."[16]

Bakunin's enthusiasm for Hegelian philosophy took him to the University of Berlin in order that he might deepen his self-acquired philosophical knowledge. Thus, his Hegelian period had an extension in Germany.

During his Russian period, Bakunin's interests were not limited to German idealistic philosophy. This received his great enthusiasm, and his attitude toward other phenomena of intellectual life was different, but they did not fail to leave an impress. Bakunin's acquaintance with them was not unimportant, since many of his later views were erected upon a basis already constructed in Russia.

Through his connection with Herzen's circle, Bakunin obtained at least a very superficial acquaintance with the ideas of Fourier and Saint-Simon. We have already seen his condemnation of Saint-Simonism in his preface to the translation of Hegel's *Gymnasialreden.*

One of the members of his own circle (the Stankevich circle), K. Aksakov, was the harbinger of a strange blend of conservatism and anarchism. Aksakov denied that Russia had benefited from the reforms of Peter the Great and objected to statism in general in regard to the Russian peasant communities (*mir*). He claimed that, unlike the West, Russia had neither slavery nor liberalism, but that nonetheless Russia was a free country. He felt that instead of a constitution what was needed was a moral identification between the government and the people, and that any legal sanction is an evil.[17]

---

[15] Bakunin, *Works,* Steklov ed., I, 405, 408.

[16] *Ibid.,* I, 174ff.

[17] Hepner, *op. cit.,* p. 70; Masaryk, *Russland und Europa,* Vol. I, Ch. X, pp. 209-293.

In Aksakov's ideas, we see the first germ of Bakunin's later political anarchism. In 1867, Bakunin wrote, "Even at that time [in the late thirties], Konstantin Sergeevich [Aksakov] and his friends were enemies of the Petersburg state and of statism in general, and in this attitude he even anticipated us."[18]

Bakunin was an omnivorous reader. In addition to theology, he had a special interest in history, though of course philosophy was his absorbing passion. At that time, he read the dogmatics of the Hegelian Marheinecke (*Die Grundlagen der Christlichen Dogmatik als Wissenschaft*, Berlin, 1827), and probably also the history of Lutheranism by the same author as well as Neander's history of the church, and Salwador's works on early Christianity and Judaism. Surprisingly, we also find on the list of Bakunin's books those of the mystics, Carl Eckartshausen and Louis Claude St. Martin, which clearly reveal the mystical inclinations of young Bakunin. Hepner states that Bakunin had a vocation for becoming a mystical thinker, but that these tendencies broke down later.[19] Perhaps Bakunin's most important new discovery was Strauss' *Life of Jesus*, which he singles out in his *Confession* to the tsar as having brought him "strong and general excitement."[20] He also read the *Hallische Jahrbücher*, and here first learned to know the name of Ludwig Feuerbach. Thus, before he left Russia, he had become aware that the Hegelians in Germany had split into left and right wings.

However, he concentrated his reading on the works of the right Hegelians: Göschel, Rosenkranz, Schaller, Hinrichs. He also tried to read the classics, Locke, Helvetius, Herder, Kant, and Schelling, as well as secondary philosophical authors such as Kiesewetter and Krug. His occupation with the romantic philosophers, such as Kreuzer and Baader, is no less interesting. Bakunin studied the history of philosophy from the texts of Reinhold, Erdmann, Michelet, and Schaller. Among the historians, he read the works of Heeren, Rotteck, Luden, Raumer, and Leo, and also Guizot's *Histoire de la civilisation en France*.[21]

Thus, Bakunin's reading was not limited to philosophy. He also had some notions about French utopian socialism, German philosophical radicalism, and even, from Guizot, he may have gained some presentiments of the class concept.

[18] Dragomanov, *op. cit.*, p. 201.   [19] Hepner, *op. cit.*, pp. 177ff.
[20] Polonski, *Materialy*, I, 105-106.
[21] Kornilov, *Molodye gody M. Bakunina*, pp. 524-533, 558-562; Chizhevski, *op. cit.*, p. 94; Carr, *op. cit.*, pp. 74, 75.

We have not touched on Bakunin's attitude toward official politics during his Russian period. Surprisingly enough, it is well documented that his attitude was a conformist one.[22]

Bakunin's short stay at the University of Berlin may be considered as an extension of the philosophical period of his life. He applied himself to the deepening of his knowledge of the Hegelian system, became personally acquainted with Schelling and Werder, and visited Schaller in Halle. Although at that time he remained an orthodox Hegelian and his letters of that time are full of excited mystical revelations, his temperament gave this orthodoxy a very peculiar tinge. For instance, he relates in a letter to his family that Professor Werder was very glad to see him again because he "needed to refresh himself with my recklessness."[23] Because of Bakunin's temperament, the tense political atmosphere of Germany of that time must have made a rapid impact on him. The process of Bakunin's conversion from a domestic to a political rebel was a question of only a short time. The turning point seems to have come in the winter of 1841-1842, when Bakunin was in close contact with the Hegelian left. Ludwig Feuerbach's *The Essence of Christianity,* the book which reduced the Christian religion to the natural nature of man,[24] provided a rallying point for the left Hegelians. In retrospect, Engels wrote of this time: "For the moment, we were all Feuerbachians." Feuerbachism provided the footbridge over which, by fairly rapid degrees, Bakunin reached politics and revolution. His godfather in this was Arnold Ruge, whose acquaintance Bakunin made in Dresden in 1841. Although at first Bakunin was slightly shocked by Ruge's radicalism and materialism, within a year he had surpassed his teacher,[25] as was proved by his article, *Reaction in Germany,* which was printed in October, 1842, in Ruge's *Deutsche Jahrbücher,* under the pseudonym of Jules Elysard. In this brilliant essay, generally acknowledged as Bakunin's best literary contribution, he, at one stroke, turned the respectable Hegelian system into, as Herzen said, an algebra of revolution. In this article, Bakunin declared "the passion for destruction to be a creative passion."

[22] Kornilov, *Molodye Gody,* p. 574; Steklov, *op. cit.,* I, 57; Carr, *op. cit.,* p. 80; Hepner, *op. cit.,* p. 97.
[23] A. A. Kornilov, *Gody stranstvii M. Bakunina* (Moscow, 1925), p. 84.
[24] K. Löwith, *Von Hegel bis Nietzsche* (Zurich, 1941), pp. 457-466.
[25] Chizhevski, *op. cit.,* p. 106.

Bakunin's final push toward revolutionism came from his study of Lorenz von Stein's *Socialism and Communism in Contemporary France* (1841). This book thoroughly explained to him for the first time the theories of Saint-Simon and Fourier, of Proudhon and Pierre Leroux. With regard to this book, Bakunin wrote in his *Confession*: "It opened to me a new world into which I plunged with all the ardor of a delirious thirst. Now I started to read all the writings of the French democrats and socialists, and swallowed all I could get in Dresden."[26] The utopian schemes of French Socialists seemed to Bakunin concrete and practical in comparison with German metaphysics. Even Feuerbach became for him "unreal and purely theoretical."[27]

Now Bakunin's retreat from philosophy became a rout. It is true that this exodus was accomplished in the company of a number of others. For instance, Bakunin related to his brother, Paul, and to Ivan Turgenev (November, 1842) that A. Ruge "has become completely free of the theoretical fog in which he was caught for so long, and he sees reality in all its pitiful nakedness."[28] This applied in an even greater degree to Bakunin himself. A few months earlier (February 21, 1842) he had written: "The era of theory has passed." A letter to his sisters (November 4, 1842) contained the advice: "Throw theory into the fire, it only spoils life." In a letter from Paris to his brother, Paul, (March 17, 1845) he stated: "I am the same enemy of the existing reality that I was, with only the difference that I have ceased being a theoretician and finally overcome metaphysics and philosophy, and wholly, with all my soul, plunged into the practical world, into the world of real deeds and real life." Bakunin closed this pronouncement with a quotation from Herwegh's poem: "Wir haben lang genug geliebt, Wir wollen endlich hassen."[29] Chizhevski remarks that "all these deliberations show more clearly than anything that Bakunin had come out of the realm of philosophy completely."[30] It is true that as a revolutionary Bakunin frequently touched on philosophical themes. But these relapses are usually utilitarian in character. Then he arbitrarily takes from philosophical systems what he supposes fits his own political postulates. In his later years, Bakunin is not a

---

[26] Polonski, *Materialy*, I, 105-106.
[27] Carr, *op. cit.*, p. 111.
[28] Quoted in Kornilov, *Gody stranstvii M. Bakunina*, p. 201.
[29] Bakunin, *Works*, Steklov ed., I, 152, 243ff.
[30] Chizhevski, *op. cit.*, p. 112.

philosophical radical but, as Chizhevski says, "a non-philosophic and anti-philosophic nihilist."[31] At this time, Bakunin wrote that Ludwig Büchner and Karl Marx were in the trap of "metaphysic abstract thought."[32]

For Bakunin, this escape from philosophy and entrance into politics could not mean a striving for the democratization of political institutions or for social progress. For such an extremist and maximalist on principle, even before his philosophic crisis, politics could mean nothing other than the revolutionary struggle. Only in this way could he quench his thirst for "deeds."

The way to "arduous," though not always "holy," deeds stood wide open. Bakunin started on his pilgrimage to the contemporary revolutionary centers. In his time, these were Switzerland, Paris, Brussels, and London. He reached Switzerland early in 1843. After a year, he went on to Brussels, and after a few months there, he moved to Paris. He reached London only after his escape from Siberia in 1861. In regard to ideological influence, his short stay in London was on the whole without any special importance.

During these journeys, Bakunin made new acquaintances and felt the impact of new ideas. In Switzerland, he met the Vogt family and August Becker, a friend and partisan of Georg Büchner. Karl Vogt abetted Bakunin's materialism, and Becker placed his connection with the local labor movement at Bakunin's service. From Becker he must have heard something about the ideas and methods of activities of Georg Büchner. But the most important person whom Bakunin encountered in Switzerland was, without doubt, Weitling. This meeting with Weitling was one of the capital events of his life, and completed his transformation into a practical revolutionary. Although Weitling failed to convert Bakunin wholly to communism, he turned his attention toward the proletariat and the labor movement. Thus, although Bakunin denounced Weitling's brand of communism in an article in *Der Schweizerische Republikaner*, he declared that communism (which in Bakunin's usage embraced the ideology of communism and socialism, and also the labor movement) was a world problem.[33] From that time on, the Russian

---

[31] *Ibid.*   [32] Bakunin, *Works, Golos Truda* ed., I, 184, 185.
[33] Bakunin, *Works*, Steklov ed., III, 222-231. Bakunin rejected communism in the following words:
  "Once and for all we announce that we are not communists. We have as little desire as the gentlemen from the *Observer* to live in a state built

aristocrat was a servant of the international proletariat. Also, it was Weitling who, after Aksakov, gave Bakunin the second push toward anarchism. Bakunin called Weitling's *Guarantees of Harmony and Freedom* a "really remarkable book," and in a letter to Ruge quoted a passage which struck him especially. "The perfect society has no government, but only an administration, no laws, but only obligations, no punishments, but means of correction."[34]

In addition, Weitling turned Bakunin's attention toward the déclassé elements of society.[35] Weitling's scheme of revolution provided an important role for these elements, and Bakunin foresaw a similar one in his later concept of revolution.

This turn toward new ideas also brought a change in Bakunin's reading list. He started an intensive reading of the economists, particularly Smith and Say. Recommending these two to his brother, Paul, he wrote: "Now I occupy myself only with them . . . ."[36]

In Brussels, Bakunin established close contact with the Polish émigrés who were conspiring against Russia. This was probably the first time that he actually came into touch with the arcana of conspiracy, his hobby of later years. But of much greater importance were his long discussions with the leader of the Polish group in Brussels, Professor J. Lelewel. Lelewel was one of the first to stress the idea of the Slav agrarian commune (under the influence of Herder and Rousseau). Hepner says that Lelewel's *Revolutionary Manifesto to the Russians* was the first outline of revolutionary Pan-Slavism. Hepner believes that, although there is little reason to think that Bakunin took the idea of federalism, which was widespread at the time, from Lelewel, there are convincing grounds for thinking that Lelewel gave Bakunin the inspiration for his revolutionary Pan-Slavism.[37]

In Paris, the formulation of Bakunin's revolutionary attitude was completed. At the time of Bakunin's arrival, Paris was an arena of lively ideological contest. It was a melting pot of social and political theories. Here, Bakunin met *en masse* the revolutionary atmosphere which suited his temperament so well.

according to Weitling's plan, one which is not the expression of a free society, but rather a herd of animals organized by compulsion and force and concerned solely with material interests, ignoring the spiritual side of life." (p. 227)

[34] Carr, *op. cit.*, p. 122.   [35] Steklov, *op. cit.*, I, 144.
[36] *Ibid.*, p. 103.   [37] Hepner, *op. cit.*, pp. 225ff.

His extremism was soon expressed in prophecies of the speedy downfall of the existing order. In a letter of that period, A. Ruge writes, "If Bakunin should be right and the world become communist within three months . . . ."[38] In Bakunin's defense, it must be said that he was not alone in having such ideas. Such prognoses were in keeping with the general revolutionary mood. There was a feeling of exaltation among the radical circles, and an expectation of the early downfall of the existing order. This fit Bakunin's innate propensity toward exaggeration. In this context, one thinks of Herzen's remark that, in regard to revolution, Bakunin always mistook the second month of pregnancy for the ninth.

In Paris, Bakunin renewed his contacts with German radicals. In addition to his acquaintance with Ruge and Herwegh, he made that of Marx, Engels, and Hess. He contributed to the revived *Deutsch-Französische Jahrbücher* of Ruge. In an article there, he completely reversed his attitude toward French philosophy, in contradistinction to his condemnation in the preface to Hegel's *Gymnasialreden*. Now he praised French 18th century philosophy, but to philosophy in general he allocated only the role of destroying superstition. During this period, he also became a contributor to the German weekly *Vorwärts*, which was edited in Paris by G. Bernstein.

In the autumn of 1844, Bakunin reported in a letter that he had "made much progress, become a Frenchman, and worked diligently on his work on the *Exposé et développement des idées de Feuerbach*."[39] Nothing further was ever heard of this project, though Bakunin maintained a lifelong admiration for Feuerbach, whom he called "one of the most daring and sympathetic thinkers of our day."[40]

However, Bakunin's contacts with the German radicals were rather on the decline. Marx and Engels had just begun to elaborate their doctrine of "scientific socialism," and Bakunin could not fall under their spell at that time. The French radicals and socialists had a much greater attraction for Bakunin. His German colleagues made the introductions, and Bakunin soon met almost every representative of "what passed for advanced

---

[38] P. Nerrlich, ed., *Arnold Ruges Briefwechsel und Tagebuchblätter* (Berlin, 1886), I, 370.
[39] Bakunin, *Works*, Steklov ed., III, 273.
[40] Bakunin, *Gesammelte Werke*, I, 245.

thought in the Paris of the forties."[41] He visited two authors whose writings had recently given him sincere delight, Lamennais and George Sand. He also met Pierre Leroux and called on Cabet. He made the acquaintance of Louis Blanc and Felix Pyat. He witnessed the development of the schools of Saint-Simon and Fourier and the conspiracy of the secret societies of the Blanquists. At that time, he probably became acquainted with the views of Babeuf, through reading Buonarotti's *"Conspiration pour l'égalité dite de Babeuf.*

At this stage of Bakunin's development, the most congenial, and perhaps the most important, influence was that of Pierre-Joseph Proudhon. The friendship between Bakunin and Proudhon became close; each influenced the other in a complex fashion. Outwardly, the similarity between the method of reasoning and the thought content of the two great anarchists is far-reaching. The views of both never become fixed, and undergo constant revision and reformulation. Both present their ideas in passionate sermons, using outrageous, vitriolic words in their outbursts. Neither shows any respect for terminology; their doctrines are therefore full of inconsistencies and are sometimes difficult to perceive. Both take refuge in bombast as a substitute for systematic, disciplined reasoning. Both deal more readily in negations, and their attacks are directed against the same objects: the state, religion, and property. Both recommend "social revolution" as a means of escape from the intolerable social situation, and both place great hopes in federalism. While a more profound analysis discovers far-going discrepancies between them, it must be stressed that it was due to the influence of Proudhon's ideas that Bakunin's instinctive rebellionism was transformed into a formulated, doctrinaire, anarchist creed. It was Proudhon who provided Bakunin with the theorems and concepts which were essential to him in his later creation of a species of anarchist doctrine, when this became necessary for Bakunin in his duel with Marx. But it took almost twenty years for Bakunin to finally accept and reformulate Proudhon's creed, just when the clash with Marx was becoming inevitable.

Two decades later, Bakunin was to make the following estimate of the ideological process of that time:

[41] Carr, *op. cit.*, p. 127.

Babeuf's conspiracy failed . . . . But his ideas of a socialist republic did not die with him. Taken up by his friend Buonarotti, the greatest conspirator of this century, that idea was transmitted as a sacred trust to the new generation. Owing to the secret societies . . . the communist ideas blossomed forth in the popular imagination. From 1830 to 1848 they found capable interpreters in the persons of Cabet and Louis Blanc, who definitively established revolutionary socialism.

Another socialist current, . . . a current which we should like to call doctrinaire socialism, was founded by two eminent men: Saint-Simon and Fourier.

In general, regimentation was the common passion of all the socialists except one [Proudhon], prior to 1848.

But then came Proudhon, a son of the peasants in his acts and his instinct, a hundred times more revolutionary than all the doctrinaire and bourgeois socialists . . . . Opposing liberty to authority, he boldly proclaimed himself an anarchist . . . .

This was the condition of social science prior to 1848 . . . . And when the revolution broke out in that year, socialism emerged as a powerful force.[42]

When the March Revolution arrived, however, Bakunin, the revolutionary, was not enrolled under the banner of socialism. As he later said, his socialism at that time was "purely instinctive."[43] Bakunin fought his way through the March Revolution under his own ensign—revolutionary Pan-Slavism. The theme of this essay precludes a detailed exposition of Bakunin's concept of revolutionary Pan-Slavism.[44] However, a few words must be said.

In the first place, Bakunin's revolutionary Pan-Slavism was a program of frantic destruction. It must be stressed that, by the time of the March Revolution, Bakunin's scheme of revolution was already formulated and that it remained unchanged in its general outlines to the end of his days. It was only the ideological rationalizations for the concept of revolution which were changed. In this respect, Bakunin provides us with an interesting example.

In the second place, Bakunin's Pan-Slavism was also a

42 Bakunin, *Works, Golos Truda* ed., III, 137-139
43 Bakunin, *Gesammelte Werke*, III, 211.
44 See B. P. Hepner, *Bakunin et le panslavism révolutionnaire;* also Hans Kohn, *Pan-Slavism* (Notre Dame, 1953), pp. 74-83.

program for the political reconstruction of eastern Europe along federalist, or rather confederalist, lines, without any traces of essentially anarchic elements. Yet, remotely, his Pan-Slavism was also a dim program for a new social order.

The manifesto of Bakunin's Pan-Slavism was his *Appeal to the Slavs,* published in the fall of 1848, which was a thundering summons to the Slavs to take the road of revolution. If so:

> In Moscow the star of Revolution will rise high and beautiful, out of the ocean of blood and fire, and it will become the guidepost for the happiness of all liberated mankind.[45]

Bakunin's Pan-Slav period of activity had an extension after his escape from Siberia. At that time, it degenerated ideologically into anti-Germanism. Bakunin stated:

> In the negative sense, Pan-Slavism is hatred of the Germans . . . . Speaking positively, Pan-Slavism is belief and assurance in the future of the Slavs: friendship, the prevalence of the village over the town, the rural way of life over the urban, and a general boundless love of liberty and the patriarchal community. Germany is our natural enemy, and the Austrian Kingdom represents a negative degeneration of the German way of life.[46]

As we have seen, Bakunin's Pan-Slavism had strong messianic elements. However, it proved to be a blind alley, and then Bakunin abandoned it ruthlessly.

Now the anarchist period of Bakunin's life was slowly approaching, the last decade of his eventful revolutionary career. Its approach was marked by another tide of new ideas. However, the wave of ideas was less motley than the previous one. This is probably due to the fact that the era of great rival philosophic and politico-social systems was slowly passing away. Bakunin's doctrine of anarchism was built within the framework of socialism. With the March Revolution, socialism entered the stage of maturity and fell under the incontestable influence of Marx and Engels. Therefore, the rivalry between Marx and Bakunin was no impediment to the fact that during his anarchist period the greatest influence on Bakunin was his chief antagonist. It may not only be said that Bakunin's doctrine of anarchism was completed and ripened in the clash with Marx-

[45] "Appeal to the Slavs" in Bakunin, *Works, Golos Truda* ed., III, 59 ff.
[46] Quoted in V. Polonski, *Mikhail A. Bakunin* (Moscow, 1920), pp. 29-31.

ism, but even that, despite this clash, it was largely constructed upon the basis of Marxism. Although one can scarcely say what form Bakunin's ideology would have taken without the impact of Marxism, there is no question that it would have been completely different. Perhaps it would have ossified in the Pan-Slavic stage. Of course, this is mere vague speculation. What is certain is that during his anarchist period the strongest influence on Bakunin was that of Marxism.

In addition, Bakunin was impressed by Comte's positivist philosophy and by Darwinism. In fact, Comte was the chief philosophical influence on Bakunin during his last decade. Bakunin, like so many, chose to use Darwinism as a proof of materialism.[47] His reading list was, as always, extensive. The best known authors on it were John Stuart Mill, Lassalle, and Schopenhauer. The interest in Schopenhauer came chiefly in Bakunin's last years. His relatively long stay in Italy, the classic country of the Carbonari tradition, served to reaffirm his belief in the apparent expediency of conspiracy.

As this sketchy presentation shows, the impact of alien ideas on Bakunin was immense. In his heated mind, they fused in strange proportions, frequently losing their original meaning. For this reason, the solution of the problem of the genealogy of Bakunin's thought—so important for an understanding of his teaching because of the eclectic character of his doctrine—remains a difficult task. Our doubt is removed only in regard to the main influences: those were Hegel, or rather Hegelianism in its left extension, Proudhon, and Marx.

With regard to Hegelianism, the following fact must be stressed. Bakunin traveled the road toward political radicalism in the company of the left Hegelians, departing from Hegelian premises, even if interpreted unorthodoxly. Bakunin himself made an important contribution to this development with his *Reaction in Germany*. His intention was not to reject the Hegelian system in general, but rather to apply its dialectics to reality. The use of Hegel as a point of departure was not fortuitous. H. Marcuse states:

> Hegel's philosophy is indeed what the subsequent reaction termed it, a negative philosophy. It is originally motivated by the conviction that the given facts that appear to common sense as the positive index of truth

[47] Masaryk, *op. cit.*, III, 3.

are in reality the negation of truth, so that truth can only be established by their destruction. The driving force of the dialectical method lies in this critical conviction. Dialectic in its entirety is linked to the conception that all forms of being are permeated by an essential negativity, and that this negativity determines their content and movement.[48]

Perhaps this is the reason that Bakunin saw his *actionisme* in the framework of Hegel's dialectics, and that he attributed to himself, in this declining world, the mission of the carrier of the antithesis in the dialectical process, of negation, i.e., of destruction.[49]

During all of his revolutionary career, Bakunin gave deeds precedence over intellectual constructions. It can scarcely be doubted that this attitude was rooted in his reading of Fichte and the romantics, of whom Bakunin was enraptured in his youth. Nevertheless, the influence of Hegel must have been much stronger, and it is better documented. In Bakunin's later writings, we find scarcely a mention of Fichte, while references to Hegel are relatively frequent. They are usually critical, to be sure, but sometimes they are joined to an acknowledgement that Hegel was the greatest philosopher of his century.[50] Bakunin's attempts to make use of Hegel's dialectics in constructing his political postulates are obvious.

In this connection, we must mention Cieszkowski's *Prolegomena zur Historiosophie,* published in Berlin in 1838. In this study, Cieszkowski, a Polish philosopher and economist, was the first, although he was a right Hegelian, to try to convert Hegel's system into a philosophy of action. For Hegel's quadrinomial division of history, he substituted a threefold one.

As antiquity was a time of premonition, of perceptivity, the modern age is one of knowledge, of consciousness, of philosophy. In the future, in place of the speculative epoch comes the productive. Mankind shall pass from reflection on the necessities of history to the creation, to the making of history.

According to Cieszkowski, we find ourselves at the door of the third systematic period, the period of deeds, which will overcome the onesidedness of the first. Thus the third period

[48] Herbert Marcuse, *Reason and Revolution* (London-New York-Toronto, 1941, pp. 26-27.
[49] Chizhevski, *op. cit.,* p. 109; Hepner, *op. cit.,* pp. 179-180.
[50] Bakunin, *Gesammelte Werke,* I, 269.

must be opened by a new migration of peoples, opposite in direction to the first: the flooding of the barbarians by the civilized peoples. For the individual it is a question of raising the will to the same elevation which human reason has already reached.

Here, of course, Cieszkowski's thought approaches close to Fichte's concept of the will as the synthesis of being and thought. According to Cieszkowski, the practicing, the active, spirit is not, as in Hegel, a derivative of the theoretical, but separate, specific, even the highest stage of the spirit.[51]

We find an extensive reflection of Cieszkowski's reasoning in Bakunin's philosophy of life; even Bakunin's stress on "barbarism" as a renewing factor of humanity is an echo of Cieszkowski, though we do not find any mention of Cieszkowski's book in Bakunin's writings. Still, there are good reasons for believing that Bakunin was acquainted with Cieszkowski's views. The *Prolegomena* was well known among the left Hegelians, and accepted with enthusiasm. Under its influence, Moses Hess wrote his *La Triarchie européenne*. Bakunin's professor of philosophy at the University of Berlin, Werder, corrected Cieszkowski's book. Herzen had already read it in Russia and remarked in his diary: "In all essentials I agree with the author astonishingly."[52] Stankevich, the leader of the philosophical circle to which Bakunin belonged, took Cieszkowski's book as the theme of his last letter to Bakunin.[53] Proudhon also knew Cieszkowski and his views, and was influenced by his economic theory.[54]

After Hegelianism, which, in one interpretation or another, had branded Bakunin's thought indelibly, Proudhon had a basic ideological influence on Bakunin. This influence was bilateral and complex. Sometimes Bakunin seemed to regard Proudhon as his disciple rather than his teacher.[55] But if he sometimes said this privately, in his writings he described himself as extending Proudhon's ideas.

As we mentioned already, superficially there appears to be

[51] W. Kühne, *Graf August Cieszkowski, ein Schüler Hegels und des deutschen Geistes* (Leipzig, 1938), pp. 25-42.

[52] Hepner, *op. cit.*, pp. 161, 162

[53] A. A. Kornilov, *Molodye gody M. Bakunina*, p. 657.

[54] Karl Diehl, *P. J. Proudhon, seine Lehre und sein Leben* (Jena, 1890), pp. 234-237.

[55] Steklov, *op. cit.*, I, 199.

considerable similarity between the Russian and the French
anarchists. Proudhon boldly attacked property, the state, and
religion; he rejected communism, preached federalism, and
talked about the universal social revolution; all these elements
also appear in Bakunin's concepts. And the bravado of Proudhon's language was similar to that of Bakunin. Hence, writers
such as Gide and Rist, in their popular *History of Economic
Doctrines*, state that Bakunin's views are a simple repetition
of Proudhon's thought, borrowed mostly from his *The General
Idea of Revolution in the 19th Century*.[56]

However, when we reach the essence of Proudhon's con-
fusing thought, the similarity diminishes. Proudhon's ideas were
not as radical as his form of expression was violent. Their meaning is more moderate than it appears to be at first glance. With
Bakunin, the opposite is true. Proudhon, for instance, attacked
only "the sum total of property abuses," but not property as
such. He was also a defender of the laws of inheritance.
Bakunin rejected both, and his proposed abolition of inheritance
played an important role in his theory. Proudhon's atheism,
though often expressed in virulently blasphemous language,
was more genuinely an attack on clericalism. He was indifferent
to the question of the existence of God.[57] Here again, Bakunin
differed. Proudhon strongly opposed the use of violence, the
idea of class war or violent revolution. He wrote: "Far from
me—all ferment of hatred and civil war. It is well enough known
that I am not what is called 'a man of action'."[58] Instead,
Proudhon developed his concept of "mutualism," which was
the backbone of his system. In all these questions, Bakunin's
position was just the opposite. The idea of class war was the
cornerstone of his doctrine; violent revolution was its pinnacle;
and Proudhon's mutualism was bluntly rejected. It may even be
doubted whether Bakunin's federalism and rejection of communism were developed under Proudhon's immediate influence.

[56] Charles Gide and Charles Rist, *A History of Economic Doctrines from the
Time of the Physiocrats to the Present Day* (London, Toronto, 1948), p.
615.
  In addition, we see that both anarchist ideologists had strong tendencies toward Judeophobia. As E. Silberner says, in this respect Proudhon "was moderate in comparison with Bakunin." The two developed
this inclination independently. ("Proudhon's Judeophobia," by E. Silberner, in *Historia Judaica*, Vol. I, No. 1, New York, 1948).
[57] Henri de Lubac, S.J., *The Un-Marxian Socialist* (London, 1948), p. 181.
[58] S. Y. Lu, *The Political Theories of J. P. Proudhon* (New York, 1922), pp.
97, 105, 137.

Proudhon developed at length his theory of federalism in his *Du Principe Fédératif*, published in 1852. In the forties, he was not an advocate of federalism.[59] Bakunin was already a herald of a ready-made federalistic program during the March Revolution. However, there is no doubt that his later pleas in favor of federalism were reinforced by Proudhon. Bakunin's rejection of communism also took place several years before he met Proudhon.

However, Bakunin was undoubtedly indebted to Proudhon for his rejection of the phenomenon of authority and of the institution of the state. Proudhon, more than any other, was responsible for transforming Bakunin's instinctive revolt against authority into a conscious anarchist creed, even though Bakunin did not identify himself with this creed until two decades after becoming acquainted with it. This adoption of Proudhon's ideas was of fundamental importance, since the rejection of any legal authority is the starting point for the entire anarchist doctrine. However, if we reduce the outward similarity of the two doctrines to their proper essence, and disregard their common outrageousness of expression, we come to the conclusion that Proudhon's influence on Bakunin was not as all-embracing as it has generally been considered. We may say with Henri de Lubac that Proudhon's thought "is nevertheless very different from that of the Russian anarchist with whom too close a parallel has often been made."[60]

Whereas the importance of Proudhon's influence on Bakunin has commonly been overemphasized, that of Marx, or rather of Marxism, has usually been underestimated. It was, however, profound. In the first place, it was only in the collision with Marx, in the First International, that Bakunin felt himself compelled to declare himself a representative of doctrinal anarchism. Previously, he had only been a disciple of revolt, without any dogma in the proper sense of this word. Such an attitude was quite proper for an anarchist, since the central content of anar-chism is the indignation of the human being against oppression. This indignation, as a reaction against any specific human situation, may evoke an action which need not be considered as an emanation of any ideology. Bakunin abandoned this position

---

[59] Lu, *op. cit.*, p. 122; cf. also Diehl, *P. J. Proudhon*, p. 115.
[60] H. de Lubac, *op. cit.*, p. 174.

under the impact of his conflict with Marx,[61] and proceeded to establish his own ideology of anarchism. In this, he used in part Proudhon's teaching, with which he had long been acquainted.

On this point, Max Adler states:

> The differentiation between socialism and anarchism developed clearly and along party lines after Bakunin's opposition to Marx's International, and even then it did not yet mean a difference in aims, but here only in the means to this end, in the tactics and the forms of the proletarian movement.[62]

Bakunin's unconditional identification with anarchism was preceded by his full participation in the labor movement. This was under the influence of Marx's example—Bakunin considered his ideology of anarchism as only a species of socialist doctrine. According to his own statements, he used Marx's historical materialism in the elaboration of his anarchist creed. In *Statism and Anarchy*, he wrote:

> In spite of all his efforts to stand on firm ground, Proudhon has remained an idealist and metaphysician. His point of departure is the abstract idea of right; from right he proceeds to economic facts. Marx, in contrast to Proudhon, has spoken out and proved the incontestable truth, confirmed by the entire past and present history of human society, peoples and states, that economic fact has always preceded juridical and political right. The presentation and proof of this constitutes one of the main scientific merits of Marx.[63]
>
> It is a great and fertile thought which he did not absolutely invent, it was glimpsed, expressed in part by

[61] Even during the most intense moments of Bakunin's conflict with Marx, he retained and admitted publicly his sincere admiration for Marx's devotion to the labor movement, the greatest respect for the latter's talents, and an awareness of the importance of Marx's theoretical achievements. Bakunin stated that "Marx is the foremost economic and socialist scholar of our time." Bakunin was the first Russian to begin a translation of *Das Kapital*, and while he usually termed this book "too abstract," he also called it "an excellent opus . . . which contains, in my opinion, a profound and clear, a scientific and decisive, and, if I may express myself in this way, an inexorable and unmasking analysis of the formation of bourgeois capital . . ." And in a letter to Marx of December 22, 1868, Bakunin absolutely called himself "your disciple." (Bakunin, *Gesammelte Werke*, III, 187; I, 213; III, 123.)

[62] Max Adler, *Die Staatsauffassung des Marxismus* (Vienna, 1922), pp. 247-248.

[63] Bakunin, *Works, Golos Truda* ed., I, 196.

> many before him; but in the last resort his is the honor
> of having established it solidly and of having set it down
> as the basis of all economic systems. On the other hand,
> Proudhon understood and felt liberty better than he.[64]

Marx's historical materialism, which Bakunin used and interpreted in a peculiar and sometimes very arbitrary way,[65] led Bakunin to the acceptance of the Marxian concept of class war. Therefore, as A. Gray concedes, "So far as Bakunin's analysis of existing society is concerned, it cannot be said that he differs materially from what is the core of the Marxian position."[66]

In addition, it was under the influence of Marxism that Bakunin accepted the idea of the abolition of private ownership of capital and land. This led him to depict the future anarchist order in a way identical with the essense of the communist ideal, with the important exception that Bakunin rejected the Marxian concept of the transitional period of the dictatorship of the proletariat, with all the means of production controlled by the new proletarian state.

Under the impact of Marxism, Bakunin developed an idea of an anarchist communist order unique among the ideologies of his anarchist predecessors or contemporaries. In his schemes, collective elements and factors clearly prevail over those of an individualistic nature. Hence, Max Stirner's *Solipsismus* was substantially different from Bakunin's ideas, although Engels expressed the view that Stirner, whom Bakunin knew personally, influenced him.[67]

It was due to Marxism that Bakunin became the founder of the communistic or collectivistic current of anarchism.

[64] Bakunin, *Gesammelte Werke*, III, 116-117.
[65] As a rule, Bakunin dilutes Marx's historical materialism to a point where it becomes little more than an insistence that the economic factor is one of the important causes of social change. In supporting his own views with arguments drawn from Marxism, Bakunin combined them with arguments which, by their very nature, often cancel out the former (e.g. racial arguments). See Bakunin, *Gesammelte Werke*, III, 244ff.
[66] Gray, *op. cit.*, p. 353.
[67] In his *Ludwig Feuerbach*, Engels stated that "Bakunin blended him [Stirner] with Proudhon and labeled the outcome 'anarchism'," (Engels, *Ludwig Feuerbach and the Outcome of Classical Philosophy*, London, 1941, p. 52). A similar view is expressed by E. H. Carr (*Michael Bakunin*, p. 434). But in his *Statism and Anarchy* Bakunin himself says of Stirner: "To this circle also belonged the brothers Bruno and Eduard Bauer and Max Stirner; at that time the leading circle of German nihilists in Berlin far surpassed in cynicism the most glaring nihilists of Russia." (Bakunin, *Works, Golos Truda* ed., I, 195.)

Yet we find a noticeable similarity between Bakunin's ideas and those of other radical political thinkers, for example Babeuf or even Godwin. At some points, the coincidence of Bakunin's views with those of Babeuf is striking. This is doubtless not fortuitous, since Bakunin had become acquainted with Babeuf's ideas through the writings of Buonarotti. In his writings and speeches, Bakunin often referred to Buonarotti, whose book he recommended to his friends.[68] The distant echoes of Godwin are not, probably, to be attributed to any Godwinian influence, but to be considered as the natural outcome of the anarchist view.[69]

---

[68] Bakunin, *Gesammelte Werke*, II, 255.
[69] Gray, *op. cit.*, p. 353.

CHAPTER 4

THE CRITIQUE OF THE EXISTING ORDER

HISTORIC anarchism of the 19th century, as elaborated by William Godwin, Pierre-Joseph Proudhon, Michael Bakunin, and Peter Kropotkin, challenged not only the state, or the rule of a given class, but the very idea of domination. This was the central point of their reasoning and action. By the term anarchism, we understand the anarchist political movement and its socio-political doctrine. Today, the historic anarchism of the 19th century is dead. The anarcho-syndicalism which bloomed in the Romanic countries during the first part of the 20th century was grounded in the clash between Communism, Fascism, and the state during the period between the two World Wars.

Certain preliminary remarks are needed to clear away misunderstandings which might arise in an exposition of anarchist doctrine. In common parlance, anarchism connotes a collective name for individual arbitrary action, willfulness, licentiousness, and the law of the jungle. The name of anarchist is commonly associated with certain conceptions of specific revolutionary tactics, manifested in direct action, individual terror, assassination by the bombing of heads of states, and terrorist conspiracy.

The theoreticians of anarchism took a remarkably different position. The anarchist ideologists of the 19th century were convinced that the absence of government which they postulated need not be identical with chaos in the sense of the war of each against all, with self-destruction, lack of order in the widest meaning of this word, or with the reign of willfulness. Quite the contrary, the leading theoreticians of anarchism were convinced that the realization of anarchist postulates would bring a new order of higher harmony to society.[1]

[1] See Chapter XV, "Exkursus über den Anarchismus," in Max Adler, *Die*

Therefore, anarchist teaching had to answer two different questions. The first problem was the critique of the existing order, based on domination, and advocacy of overthrowing it by way of revolution. The second was that of formulating and establishing an anarchist order without domination.

In limitation of this, it must be said that anarchist thought also aimed in part at a positive attitude toward the factual situation of disorder. Therefore, the introduction of anarchy in the sense of disorder was sometimes advocated when this appeared to be the only way out of an intolerable situation, one which had to be ended even if it were not known how anarchy would operate.

For fundamental reasons, anarchist thinkers solved the two problems which they posed themselves very unequally. The central core of anarchism is created by the indignation of the human being against any oppression. Therefore, it is primarily a case of human-moral reaction, and not of a particular theoretical or ideological conviction. An anarchist is, in his own judgment, a rebel rather than a revolutionary, since by a rebel we mean an insurrectionist without a dogma.[2]

This was the approach of historic anarchism, and therefore, the critical part was given particular attention and rendered independent of the prescription. On the other hand, anarchist teaching was unable to deliver a multilateral positive solution of social, economic, and cultural problems. Indeed, the anarchists frequently denied the expediency of enunciating theoretical solutions. According to this view, an anarchist revolution did not require the previous elaboration of a positive program. Although an anarchist does not identify anarchy with suicidal chaos, he is unable to draw concrete outlines of the future order. This is the reason that the origin and emphasis of anarchism lie in the analysis of domination and of the ways for its overthrow. The concrete answer to the problem of anarchy was to be transferred to the realm of practical experiment, which could start only after a successful anarchist revolution. Therefore, from its origin, anarchism became a moral way of action in a given human situation rather than a scientific recognition of a determined historic causality.[3]

Staatsauffassung des Marxismus; R. Stammler, *Die Theorie des Anarchismus* (Berlin, 1894).

[2] Peter Heintz, *Anarchismus und Gegenwart* (Zurich, 1951), pp. 18-24.

[3] *Ibid.*, p. 16.

In general, these remarks apply to Bakunin's anarchist doctrine. However, one reservation must be made, one which had important consequences for Bakunin's reasoning. He attempted to reconcile his anarchism with materialism, positivism, historical dialectics, Darwinism, and Marxism. These attempts at reconciliation were far-reaching, and, in Bakunin's mind, these systems provided the real basis for his anarchism. His desire to pin his ideological conclusions to these doctrines is manifest at every step, and he was continually willing to take refuge with the self-confident creators of these doctrines.

This circumstance, it seems, is the main source of the inconsistency and contradiction in Bakunin's reasoning, for all these theoretical concepts do not match his main problem—revolution. In his usual uncompromising fashion, Bakunin declared himself an adherent of materialism, and even reproached Marx and Ludwig Büchner for apparent inconsistencies in this line.[4] To Bakunin, only two philosophical systems were possible: materialism and idealism. What is not consonant with one, must belong to the other. The former, materialism, is the only true one; the second, idealism, is false, and owes its origin and popularity to the same source that superstition does. Hence, according to Bakunin: "Theology is the science of the divine lie, jurisprudence the science of the human lie, and metaphysics and idealistic philosophy the science of any half-lie."[5]

For Bakunin, psychology and history are materialistic. As a consequence, he had to accept a complete naturalistic determinism. On the basis of this materialist determinism, Bakunin denied that free will operated in breaking the law, especially criminal law. The individual is an involuntary product of nature and the social milieu, from which kings and criminals emerge in exactly the same fashion. In order to punish criminals, society takes refuge in a belief in individual responsibility. However, according to Bakunin, such a theory is derived from theology, and is a combination of absurdity and hypocrisy. He traced this immorality to political, social, and economic inequality. This inequality was to vanish with the achievement of the revolution.[6]

If everything is determined by the world reality, what is the place of the free human agent so indispensable to anarchist

---

[4] Bakunin, *Works, Golos Truda* ed., I, 184-185.
[5] *Ibid.*, IV, 31.
[6] Bakunin, *Gesammelte Werke*, III, 81.

rebellionism? Bakunin tried to find a remedy by defining the notion of matter as vaguely as possible. But since even this did not always bring him the desired solution, he took refuge in the notions of "nature" and "life" which he made to contain everything. However, by this procedure, scarcely anything except the phraseology was left of all the above-mentioned systems. To be sure, this allowed him to give an apparent justification to everything, but not to explain or perceive. Thus, despite his determinism, Bakunin gave himself pains to preserve the freedom of the individuum; on the other hand, this freedom becomes inconvenient for him, since determinism, as a cloak for political aspirations passed off as historical necessity, is of extraordinary value in making a political doctrine attractive.

In accepting Darwinism, he could not refuse evolutionism, and, consequently, he should have admitted that the attainment of political goals would be gradual, through many transitional stages. From Hegel and Comte, he drew the idea of historical laws of development in great epochs. But all this was but little in keeping with his central theme of revolution.

Bakunin made another great theoretical concession to Marxism, especially to historical materialism. Here, he encountered the same difficulties. According to Marxism, the revolutionary spirit which will achieve social goals is a function of economic development. The latter gradually and steadily brings ever larger strata of society into opposition to the existing order. Revolutionary consciousness is a corollary. Marxism sees the social revolution as coming inevitably. Anarchism (including Bakunin) believes that it can and must be made to come. According to Marxism, revolution must come by virtue of the laws of society; according to anarchism, revolution ought to come and therefore it must be made. Revolutionary consciousness is a preliminary factor which must be created. Thus, Bakunin's example proved the truth of Max Weber's words before they were said: "The materialist interpretation of history is no cab to be taken at will; it does not stop short of promoters of revolutions."[7]

As a final result of Bakunin's attempts to reinforce his doctrine of anarchism with all these systems, there came a continual vacillation between the idea of the primacy of economics and that of the basic importance of political and religious elements.

[7] Max Weber, *Essays in Sociology* (New York, 1946), p. 125.

His anarchism, torn between individualism and the negation of individuality, ended with absolutism. Bakunin had already rejected subjectivism and individualism in his preface to Hegel's *Gymnasialreden* (1838). Shortly before his death, in a talk on Schopenhauer, he condemned individualism saying:

> Our whole philosophy has a false basis if it considers man as an individual instead of as belonging to a collective body, as it should. This is the source of most of the philosophical errors which result in transferring happiness to the clouds, or in a pessimism like that of Schopenhauer and Hartmann.

Despite this condemnation of individualism, Bakunin was never able to shake off the influence of German subjectivist and individualistic philosophy. Hence, his doctrine is an amalgam of collectivism and individualism, but he was never able to formulate their interrelationship.[8]

The starting point for Bakunin's critique of the existing order was his presumption that individual freedom is the highest value.

> . . . no value exists outside freedom, and freedom is the source of and absolute precondition for any other value which really deserves this name.
> Thus value is nothing other than freedom.[9]

What Bakunin understood by liberty will be discussed in the last chapter of this essay. At this point, primarily in order to become acquainted with Bakunin's way of reasoning, we shall mention Bakunin's opinion of the "doctrinaire liberals" who, according to Bakunin, were the first to take individual liberty as the starting point for their doctrine. These theorists arrived at the conclusion that the state is a necessary evil. In practice, however, Bakunin believed that they were fanatic defenders of the absolute value of the state.[10] Bakunin posed the question of why this was the case and answered that apart from many utilitarian considerations, the reason was that they proceeded from the erroneous theoretical premise that "individual freedom is not a historical product of society," but "precedes any society, every human being bringing it with him at the time of his

---

[8] Masaryk, *op. cit.*, II, 28-29.
[9] M. A. Bakunin. *Izbrannye sochineniya (Selected Works)* (1920), p. 248.
[10] M. A. Bakunin, *Polnoye sobraniye sochinenii (Complete Collection of Works)*, I, 1. (In spite of its title, this collection contains only a small portion of Bakunin's writings.)

birth, together with his immortal soul, as a gift from God."[11]
Thus, man is posited as an "absolute being"; "according to this
liberal theory, individuals are not created by society, on the
contrary they create society itself." Hence, in Bakunin's view,
for the liberals, "society in the true meaning of the word does
not exist."[12]

In Bakunin's eyes, the real facts were entirely different.

> Beginning from the gorilla stage, it is only with great
> difficulty that man arrives at the realization of his human-
> ity and of his freedom. At the beginning he cannot have
> either this awareness or this freedom; he comes into the
> world as a wild animal and a slave. It is only in the lap
> of society, which is necessary for the development of his
> thought, his speech and his will, that he gradually be-
> comes a man and free . . . . According to the system of
> the materialists, the only natural and logical one, society
> neither limits nor diminishes freedom, but indeed first
> creates freedom for human individuals. Society is the
> root, the tree; freedom is its fruit. Therefore, in every
> age man has to seek his freedom at the end, not the begin-
> ning of history. And it may be said that the genuine and
> complete liberation of mankind is the great aim, the
> sublime end of history.[13]

After making a marginal note of how this single passage
illustrates the fusion of alien doctrinal systems (here we see
elements of Darwinism, materialism, and Hegelianism) in
Bakunin's thought, let us return to the presentation of his
reasoning.

Any limitation of freedom, says Bakunin, leads to discrimination among men; this results in domination of man over man,
and this in turn produces oppression. Since the most complete
manifestation of domination is the state, the state is the main
object of criticism of historic anarchism, and also of Bakunin.
For him, the state is the unconditional enemy of freedom.

> The state is force; nay, it is the silly parading of force.
> However many pains it may take, it cannot conceal the
> fact that it is the legal maimer of our will, the constant
> negation of our liberty. Even when it commands good,
> it makes this valueless by commanding it, for every com-
> mand slaps liberty in the face.[14]

[11] *Ibid.*, p. 2.   [12] *Ibid.*, p. 3.   [13] *Ibid.*, p. 9.   [14] *Ibid.*, pp. 17-18.

Therefore, in Bakunin's opinion, the state does not create any precondition of freedom. It is untrue that any state secures liberty. On the contrary, freedom and domination are mutually exclusive, and any political power, no matter what its source and make-up, inevitably tends toward despotism.[15]

By omitting from consideration all aspects of the state except the fundamental one of domination, Bakunin, like the other anarchists, makes a critique which is rhetorically effective but scarcely explanatory. Such an oversimplified approach pushes all the other problems connected with the institution of the state out of sight. Only one possible attitude is left, that of summary rejection. Any question of the constitution of a state becomes irrelevant.

We abhor monarchy with all our hearts. . . .[16]

But some people claim that the state, if it is a democratic one based on the free franchise of all citizens, cannot be a denial of freedom. Why not? This would depend entirely on the power of the state, which the citizens assigned to it, and on the decisions it made. A republican state, based on a general election law, can be despotic; it can even be more despotic than any monarchy. Under the pretense of representing the will of all, it may suppress the freedom and free behavior of each member, with the help of its collective might.[17]

Neither does the size or strength of the various states play any real role. "Powerful states can maintain themselves only by crime, little states are virtuous only by weakness."[18] Political power necessarily corrupts the rulers. Political domination depraves not only those who submit, but also those who execute it.[19]

From such a picture of political reality, Bakunin drew the conclusion that what was needed was a revolution which would destroy the institution of the state completely and forever.

It is necessary to abolish completely, in principle and in practice, everything which may be called political power; as long as political power exists there will always be rulers and ruled, masters and slaves, exploiters and exploited.[20]

---

[15] Bakunin, *Works, Golos Truda* ed., III, 20.
[16] Bakunin, *Selected Works,* p. 99.   [17] *Ibid.,* p. 203.
[18] *Ibid.,* p. 211.   [19] Bakunin, *Complete Collection,* II, 166.
[20] Bakunin, *Works, Golos Truda* ed., III, 22.

According to the anarchists, state sovereignty is not to be derived from the human community and its needs. Conceptually sovereignty must be bestowed upon the state by the fiction of a superior being, something outside of society. Bakunin believed this was originally the idea of God, or any religion, and also any abstract conception justifying the phenomenon of state sovereignty.

Bakunin's attitude toward religion changed radically during his life. In his youth, he manifested what may be called "secular religiosity," with mystical inclinations, all outside the church.[21] In his introduction to Hegel's *Gymnasialreden*, Bakunin developed the following idea of theocracy. "Where there is no religion, no state can exist. Religion is the substance and essence of the life of any state."[22] In 1849, obviously under the influence of Feuerbach's anthropologism, Bakunin wrote: "You are mistaken if you think that I do not believe in God . . . . I seek God in man, in human freedom, and now I seek God in revolution." During his anarchist period, Bakunin, like Proudhon, paraphrased Voltaire's well-known dictum, saying that if God exists, he must be destroyed.

Despite the diametrical opposition between his earlier and later attitude toward religion, their essence is not so dissimilar. As V. Zenkovsky says: "The search for God in revolution is not an empty phrase. This revolutionary mysticism is dialectically connected with historiosophical and religious immanentism."[23]

In his writings, Bakunin devoted a disproportionately large part of his reasoning to religious, or rather, to atheistic themes. But in spite of this plethora, there is relatively little which has any value other than that of satisfying curiosity. Most of this writing represents either commentaries on the picturesque anti-clerical aphorisms of Voltaire and Proudhon, or a raw, arbitrary accumulation of ideas and theorems taken mainly from Strauss, Feuerbach, and also Comte. Bakunin's argumentation on this problem never reaches the level of integrated reasoning. What does emerge from often reiterated, with few variations in language, denunciations of God and religion, is the integrity of his psychological attitude in this question, the intense extremism of his belligerent atheism.

[21] V. V. Zenkovsky, *A History of Russian Philosophy* (New York-London, 1953), I, 247.
[22] Bakunin, *Works*, Steklov ed., II, 172, 173.
[23] Zenkovsky, *op. cit.*, p. 257.

According to Bakunin, theism and religion in general were responsible for the deplorable contemporary social order.

> Every earthly or human authority is supposed to stem directly from the spiritual or the divine. . . . God, or rather the idea of God, is, therefore, the sanctification and the spiritual and moral cause of all slavery in the world.
>
> The state is only the younger brother of the church.[24]

This last, a dictum of Proudhon, was one which Bakunin often repeated.

Like his teachers, Bakunin considered ecclesiastical religion as a superstition born of poverty and enslavement. For him, the church was a sort of heavenly tavern, and the tavern in turn the heavenly church on earth. In both the church and the tavern, the poor man could forget his sorrows and poverty for a moment; in the former drowning them in irrational faith, and in the latter in alcohol. Bakunin did not think of religion merely as theism, but also laid great stress on the doctrine of immortality. For him, as for his predecessors, atheism was at the same time materialism in the sense of antispiritualism. In particular, Bakunin looked to Comte for a reduction of psychology to a branch of biology, one of the natural sciences.[25] He supported the ontological demonstration that: "If God exists, man is a slave; but man can and must be free, therefore God does not exist."[26]

Yet, perhaps recollecting Strauss, Bakunin acknowledged that religions developed historically and were formed by all of society. And, certainly, as a concession to historical materialism, he also agreed to consider the institution of the state as a historical necessity.[27] However, acceptance of the idea that human development follows historical laws scarcely matched Bakunin's ideological foundation of revolution. Hence, although Bakunin often touched upon this point, he never submitted it to a detailed examination.

Since, for Bakunin, no form of religion (especially Christianity) was fitted for the social and moral betterment of man, war against it and against God, or the idea of God, was a social and moral commandment. The history of mankind has been that of development through rebellion and through thought. But these weapons of humanization are characteristic of the idea

---

[24] Bakunin, *Complete Collection*, I, 14-16. [25] Masaryk, *op. cit.*, II, 16.
[26] Bakunin, *Works, Golos Truda* ed., II, 144.
[27] Bakunin, *Complete Collection*, I, 17.

of Satan. By Satan, man becomes free; by God, he chains himself to slavery. Like many of his contemporaries, Bakunin considered his time as one of transition from theological illusion to positivistic sobriety and realistic materialism. Only atheism, he believed, is able to liberate man truly. Therefore, its acceptance is an essential precondition of social transformation.

As A. Gray summarizes this, Bakunin's revolt against God (or the idea of God) and his rebellion against the state may, in a sense, be regarded as two phases of his gospel of disobedience. In his view, anarchism and atheism were practically interchangeable terms; there could be no anarchism without atheism, and no atheism without anarchism.[28]

It might seem to be appropriate to use Bakunin's Russian background as an explanation of his attitude. In contemporary Russia, Orthodox theology was at the same time the official ideology of the Russian political autocracy; whereas the Western world had experienced the Reformation and the Renaissance, Humanism, and the Age of Reason. In the West, the way toward atheistic materialism, to Feuerbach and Stirner, had passed through many successive stages. This was not true in Russia where, up to modern times, almost all spiritual life, with all its manifestations, including controversies, had revolved around Russian Orthodox theology and the Orthodox Church. Therefore, anyone who attacked theology and religion was at the same time undermining the ideological basis of the Russian state and society.

However, the close relation of church and state in Russia cannot be called the main cause of Bakunin's atheism. This was only one of many causes and certainly not the decisive one. The real bases were much more profound, and were, in fact, certainly more complex than the arguments which he was able to adduce on behalf of his atheism. Perhaps a clue may be found in the great stress which Bakunin laid on the rejection of the doctrine of immortality. Bakunin's reasoning here may perhaps be summarized as follows: The Christian doctrine of an immortal soul makes man into an absolute being, and therefore a morally independent being. Man has need of other men materially, but because of this doctrine of immortality, his approach to others can only be an egoistic one. Morally, man

28 Gray, *op. cit.*, pp. 354-355.

has no need of his fellows, and this must create a fatal split in his personality.

There are good reasons for not limiting this argument of Bakunin to the problem of immortality, but for extending it to his entire revolutionary *Weltanschauung*. In doing this, we shall reach the final causes of his atheism and see the essential importance of the latter in Bakunin's radical liturgy. He was dominated by his desire to achieve a unity of theory and practice, of fact and value, of thought and action, within the reality of a given historical social order. As we shall see, this proposed unity of thought and action, of fact and value, was to become the imperative substratum for Bakunin's concept of revolution, of the revolutionary movement, and of the futuer social order. Perhaps this is the keystone to Bakunin's atheism. Athiesm was to provide a means for removing everything which might endanger this unity. This gives Bakunin's concept of atheism a new and distinct dimension. It is by no means an attitude of indifference toward religion, and it is certainly not limited to anti-clericalism. It is a permanently aggressive attitude toward any religion with transcendent elements. If Christianity was the first object of his attack, this was not only because it was the object closest at hand, but primarily because of its doctrinal character.

In religious matters, Bakunin's goal was always the destruction of religion. But his tactics were flexible, and he often suggested various ways for achieving its destruction. He praised Marx for not including the question of attitude toward religion in the statutes of the International.[29] And he was even willing to tolerate "superstition" in the case of Russia.

> In our propaganda among the masses we shall not put the religious problem in the first place. Our first obligation . . . is economic-political, economic in the sense of social revolution, political in the sense of destroying the state. To occupy them [the people] with the religious question means drawing them away from the main task.[30]

In Bakunin's eyes, religion would finally be killed only by social revolution.

The analogy between Bakunin's attitude toward religion and that of the Bolsheviks leaps to the eyes. In Soviet Russia, the

[29] Bakunin, *Works, Golos Truda* ed., IV, 7.
[30] Bakunin, *Complete Collection*, II, 255.

slogan was forged: " No Marxism without atheism and no atheism without Marxism,"[31] and up to the late thirties the propagation of atheism took the form of an aggressive war against religion. At the same time, the tactics were flexible. Although Lenin declared that "our programme thus necessarily includes the propaganda of atheism,"[32] at the same time he also said that the Communist Party must not allow "its forces waging a genuinely revolutionary economic and political struggle to be broken up for the sake of opinions and dreams that are of third-rate importance."[33]

This far-reaching parallelism between the ideas of Bakunin and those of the Bolsheviks is not due to borrowing from the great anarchist. It was the same Russian reality and the same goals which suggested that the same way should be taken.

In connection with Bakunin's attitude toward state sovereignty, we should note that in addition to rejecting all theocratic theoretical bases for state sovereignty, he no less radically, but in immeasurably less detail, also rejected all other theories on this problem. Thus, he denounced all the concepts "of the jurists and modern writers, whether of the Kantian or other individualistic schools . . . or those of the Hegelian . . . or naturalist school."[34] In Bakunin's mind, all these theories were "secular superstitions," created with the sole aim of legalizing domination and enslavement. Within this range, his main attack was directed against Rousseau, whom Bakunin called: "the most pernicious writer of the 18th century, the sophist who inspired all the bourgeois revolutionaries,"[35] and against Rousseau's *Contrat Social*, which Bakunin condemned as a pure fiction in the historical sense.[36]

Bakunin's thought about the state and religion, as presented above, follows the classic lines of the anarchist critique of the existing social reality. It considers historical development not as a fixed course of causality but as a tension between the emancipated human spirit and petrified historic social institutions. This conception makes it possible to expect the starting of revolution at almost any historical moment which coincides well with the essence of the anarchist program.

[31] V. I. Lenin, *Religion* (New York, no date), p. 5.
[32] *Ibid.*, p. 14.   [33] *Ibid.*, p. 15.
[34] Bakunin, *Works, Golos Truda* ed., III, 184, 185.
[35] Bakunin, *Gesammelte Werke*, II, 295.
[36] Bakunin, *Works, Golos Truda* ed., III, 168 ff.

But Bakunin did not limit himself to this approach. Under the impact of historic materialism and Marxism, he made another critique of the existing social reality. This one does not differ materially from the core of the Marxian position.

The starting point for this critique by Bakunin was the concept of class war. To this, he gave considerable emphasis. Class struggle in society is inevitable,[37] it is also irreconcilable. He readily acceded to the Marxian device that: "The subordination of labor to capital is the source of all slavery: political, moral and material."[38] Moreover, he stated that "underlying all historic problems, national, religious and political, there has always been the economic problem, the most important and essential."[39]

Bakunin found that in opposition to the bourgeois class was the working class—the disinherited, deprived of capital, land, and education. The culture of the few, he felt, was based on the forced labor and relative barbarism of the many.[40] It was not merely that some live at the expense of the others, but that among the bourgeoisie, every individual is necessarily impelled to be an exploiter of others. The market is the meeting place between the drive for lucre and starvation, between master and slave.[41] Bakunin made a full application of the Lassallian iron law of wages. Property and capital exploit labor. They are iniquitous in their historic origin, and parasitic in their functioning.[42] Hence, it follows that:

> So long as property and capital exist on the one hand, and labor on the other, the former constituting the bourgeois class and the latter the proletariat, the workers will be slaves and the bourgeoisie the master.[43]

Bakunin was unable to answer the question of how "property and capital arrived in the hands of the present possessors," perhaps because Marx had said little about this problem (see *Capital,* Vol I, Ch. XXIV, "So-called Primitive Accumulation"), and ducked this dilemma by stating:

> This is a question which, from the viewpoint of history,

---

[37] G. Maximoff, *The Political Philosophy of Bakunin: Scientific Anarchism,* pp. 187ff.
[38] Bakunin, *Selected Works,* p. 265.   [39] Maximoff, *op. cit.,* p. 358.
[40] Bakunin, *Works, Golos Truda* ed., III, 134ff.
[41] Bakunin, *Gesammelte Werke,* I, 212.   [42] *Ibid.,* pp. 204-208.
[43] Maximoff, *op. cit.,* p. 181.

logic and justice, can only be decided against the posses-sors.[44]

Bakunin linked inseparably the institution of property and the state.

> The juridical idea of property, as well as that of family law, could arise historically only in the state, the first inevitable act of which was the establishment of this law and of property.[45]

According to this new approach, the state has, throughout its existence, always been the patrimony of some privileged class. Indeed, for the safety of the state it is essential that there be a privileged class which has a vital stake in its exist-ence. "Exploitation is the flesh, domination the soul, of the bourgeois state."[46] The bourgeois state is a "mutual under-standing," a "permanent conspiracy of the exploiters."[47]

So all of society is divided into two camps: the huge one of the exploited, and the relatively small one of the exploiters. Between these two there is an insurmountable gulf. Since the bourgeoisie is doomed in case of revolution, the only way for it to evade its fate would be for it to abdicate its social position voluntarily. But, says Bakunin, "the classes never have sacrificed themselves and they never will."[48] Therefore, the gulf between the two camps not only remains but, with the increasing con-centration of wealth, becomes ever wider, and the class of ex-ploiters diminishes numerically.

> This wealth is exclusive and every day tends to become increasingly so, by becoming concentrated into the hands of an ever smaller number of persons and by throwing the lower stratum of the middle class, the petty bour-geoisie, into the ranks of the proletariat. The develop-ment of this wealth is directly related to the growing poverty of the masses of workers. Hence it follows that the gulf separating the lucky and privileged minority from the millions of workers who maintain this minority through their own labor is ever widening.[49]

The urban proletariat belongs unconditionally in the camp of the exploited, since these workers do not possess the means

---

[44] Bakunin, *Gesammelte Werke*, I, 205.
[46] Bakunin, *Complete Collection*, I, 42.
[48] Bakunin, *Gesammelte Werke*, I, 168.
[49] Maximoff, *op. cit.*, pp. 182-183.

[45] Maximoff, *op. cit.*, p. 179.
[47] Maximoff, *op. cit.*, p. 179.

of production and sell their labor under conditions to which the Lassallian iron law of wages applies.

> The current price of primary necessities constitutes the prevailing constant level above which workers' wages can never rise for long, but beneath which they drop very often, which constantly results in inanition, sickness and death, until a sufficient number of workers disappear to equalize again the supply of and demand for labor.[50]

The small peasantry must soon belong to the camp of the exploited also.

> The small peasant property, weighed down by debts, mortgages, taxes, and all kinds of levies, melts away and slips out of the owners' hands, helping to round out the ever-growing possessions of the big owners; an inevitable economic law pushes him in turn into the ranks of the proletariat.[51]

As for the group of the petty bourgeoisie, Bakunin's prognosis again followed Marx's theory of social polarization.

> [The petty bourgeoisie] will gradually lose themselves in the rank of the proletariat, all this taking place as the result of the same inevitable concentration of property in the hands of an ever smaller number of people, necessarily entailing the division of the social world into a small, very rich, learned and ruling minority and the vast majority of miserable ignorant proletarians and slaves.[52]

Since Bakunin considered that the petty bourgeoisie was on the decline, he assumed that it was a potential ally of the proletariat.[53]

Although Bakunin took a rather optimistic view of the possibility of including the petty bourgeoisie within the revolutionary forces, he was rather perturbed by certain developments within the working class itself. Here, he saw the emergence of a new stratum which he called the "aristocracy of labor," and which he considered as "quite harmful" to the cause of social transformation.[54]

Up to this point, Bakunin's reasoning followed, by and large, the Marxian line of thought. He took the economic factor as

[50] *Ibid.*, p. 185.   [51] *Ibid.*, p. 183.   [52] *Ibid.*, p. 196.
[53] Bakunin, *Works, Golos Truda* ed., IV, 30.
[54] Maximoff, *op. cit.*, pp. 200ff.

the criterion for the class division of society, and stressed ownership of the means of production. From this premise, Bakunin
drew the conclusion that all private property, i.e., capital goods
and land, must be abolished. This had a basic influence on
his conception of the future anarchist order. "Collective property
and individual property, these two banners will be the standards
under which, from now on, the great battles of the future will
be fought."[55]

However, Bakunin's Marxian consistency did not go too far.
In seeking the criteria which determine class adherence, he
did not limit himself to economic factors. He also applied
criteria of another nature, showing that the social position of
an individual is not necessarily conditioned by his economic
status. Among other factors, Bakunin first stressed the effect of
education, strictly speaking of "bourgeois education," which
allows an individual to take a higher, privileged position in
society, even though he does not possess means of production.

> All these different political and social groupings may
> now be reduced to the two principal categories, diametri
> cally opposed and naturally hostile to each other: the
> political class, comprising all those who are privileged in
> respect to possession of land, capital, or even only
> bourgeois education, and the working class, disinherited
> of land as well as capital, and deprived of all education
> and instruction.[56]

Therefore, according to Bakunin, we have "plain working
people and educated society."[57] He also laid extreme stress on
the division between manual and mental labor, and in turn
is almost willing to consider the latter as usually exploiting.
Thus, by gradually abandoning economic criteria, Bakunin
simply divided society into the privileged and the non-privileged.
The definition of who belongs to which group becomes so vague
that the camp of the non-privileged comes to include all who
feel that they belong there. In this way, the psychological factor
becomes, though unavowedly, the measure for determining class
adherence. Therefore, Bakunin, in spite of adopting the Marxian critique of society, allowed himself to disregard the Marxian
theory of economic causality in human history and to avoid the

[55] Bakunin, *Gesammelte Werke*, II, 67.
[56] Bakunin, *Works, Golos Truda* ed., III, 131-132.
[57] Maximoff, *op: cit.*, p. 190.

necessity of defining the outside deterministic factors for revolution.

In summary, Bakunin's critique of existing society followed two patterns. One developed along the classic anarchist lines, starting with man's indignation against oppression. It did not regard the state, property, and religion as phenomena proper to a given historic period and did not take into account any fixed causal course of historical development. It allowed rebellion against any oppression at any suitable moment, from the individual point of view. Scarcely any objective restrictions were left on the will and action of the individual. Once a cause was morally justified, any action arising from this cause was also justified.

On the other hand, Bakunin also supported an analysis of existing reality in Marxian terms. From this basis, he drew the conclusion of the necessity of abolishing private ownership. But he disregarded the Marxian dialectical determinism of the historical process. From the premise of irreconcilable class war and exploitation, Bakunin drew the same conclusions that the later syndicalists were to draw: that any peaceful political action of the labor movement within the framework of the existing order is pointless or even harmful, and that therefore the workers must abstain from it under any conditions.[58]

In connection with Bakunin's critique of the existing society, one further question should be cleared up, that of whether Bakunin's critique of the Western capitalistic order was not preconditioned by the so-called Russian theory of "the rotten West," a view very popular among Russian intellectual circles. There were also Russian revolutionaries who, while rejecting the autocracy of the Russian political system, at the same time praised the Russian rural social system and condemned the civilization of the West. The starting point for their reasoning was the rural repartitional commune, the *mir*. The best known of the Russian radicals to take this view was Herzen, Bakunin's life-long close friend. Considering the *mir* as the basis for social renewal, Herzen stated "that which in the West can be achieved only through a series of catastrophies, can develop in Russia on the basis of what already exists."[59]

These views of the Russian radicals partially coincided with

[58] On this question see Bakunin's pamphlet, *The Policy of the International.*
[59] Quoted in E. H. Carr, *Studies in Revolution* (London, 1950), p. 70.

those of the Slavophiles, a conservative and politically conformist school of Russian thought which also took the *mir* as the starting point for its schemes. Thus, independently but not without a reciprocal influence, a parallelism developed between these radical and conservative schools. The connecting links were the *mir*, the theory of the rotten West, Russian messianism, and a negative evaluation of the reforms of Peter the Great.

Is it also true of Bakunin, as of Herzen, that the critique of the capitalistic bourgeois society was mainly conditioned by the theory of the rotten West and by approval of the Russian rural commune? Berdyaev says:

> Bakunin's philosophy of life had a strongly Slavophile tinge; his revolutionary messianism had an outspoken Russian Slavic character.[60]

This, however, is an oversimplification. In regard to this problem, as to others, Bakunin went through an extensive evolution during his lifetime, and never reached a fixed, stable attitude. During his Pan-Slavic period, he, like Herzen, considered the Russian folk as destined for making social revolution. At that time, his program showed a strongly Slavophile, messianic coloring. Thus, early in 1862, Ruge wrote to a friend about Bakunin's arrival in London:

> Bakunin has arrived. I don't know, but probably I shall see him. But he has become even more Russian than Herzen. Russian revolution makes Russians like Herzen and Bakunin even more shameless, and I expect in advance speeches about the "youthfulness of Russia" and the "decadence of Germany."[61]

However, it was not political or nationalistic Pan-Slavism, but revolutionary Slavophile messianism to which Bakunin gave his allegiance. Unlike Herzen, Bakunin stressed Slavic rather than Russian messianism. His attitude toward the *mir* was also different. Although he considered the *mir's* collective ownership of land as desirable, he energetically condemned the patriarchal system in the *mir*, since he believed that this suppressed individual freedom and prevented internal moral and economic development. According to him, the *mir* was an institution of "Chinese immobility."[62]

[60] N. Berdiajew, *op. cit.*, p. 74.   [61] A. Ruge, *Briefwechsel*, II, 217.
[62] Bakunin, *Complete Collection*, II, 256ff. Bakunin also condemned the *mir* in a letter of July 19, 1866 to Herzen, printed in Dragomanov, *op. cit.*,

Thus, Bakunin relied incomparably more on the apparent revolutionary instincts of the Russian peasant than on the institution of the *mir*. He saw the source of revolutionism, as he called it, in the "barbarism" of the peasants, and considered this stage of barbarism as almost the equivalent to aptness for making revolution. In his reveries, the Slavic masses, and especially the Russians, were innate socialists, against the institution of the state, anarchists, pacifists, anti-imperialists, and born revolutionaries. But when his revolutionary Pan-Slavism proved to be a failure, Bakunin transferred his revolutionary hopes to the Romanic peoples. He discovered revolutionary or rebellious instincts in almost every people, one after another. In an article printed in 1868, he rejected outright the doctrine of the rottenness of the West and of the messianic destiny of Russia.[63] This, however, did not mean that he was reconciled to Western social civilization, just as his previous Pan-Slavism had not meant that he recommended the Russian reality for the West. Bakunin's true position emerged out of his program of frantic revolution. This allowed him not only to reject and condemn the reality of the West, but also to ignore that of Russia.

Bakunin's preoccupation with the Slavic world did have certain important and enduring consequences. One was that, without any special realistic value, he established in his mind a scale of aptness for revolution of the various nations.

> . . . in German blood, in German instincts, in the German tradition, there is a passion for state order and state discipline . . . The Slavs not only lack such a passion, but in them completely contrary passions act and are revealed.[64]

Two other consequences of Bakunin's interest in the Slavic world are of noticeable importance. As a result of Bakunin's Russian background, he was extremely sensitive to the peasant question. With unexampled zeal, he tried to include within his doctrine of anarchism, which he considered as a species of socialism, the solution of the peasant problem, which has caused so much trouble to every socialist theoretician. He tirelessly

pp. 177ff. Later, to disavow himself decisively from the political views of Herzen, Bakunin stated: ". . . he [Herzen], no matter what Marx thinks, was never my [political] friend." (Bakunin, *Gesammelte Werke*, II, 219).
[63] Steklov, *op. cit.*, II, 360.
[64] Bakunin, *Complete Collection*, II, 52-54.

advocated the view that the peasantry is an irreplaceable revolutionary force.

A further consequence of the impact of the Slavic world on Bakunin was that for him the difference between the state and nationality was much clearer and more alive than it was for others such as Marx. Among Russian radicals and revolutionaries, it was Bakunin who, next to Lenin, paid the greatest attention to this problem, and he was incomparably more sincere than the latter. Bakunin had a remarkable influence on Russian federative thought.

CHAPTER 5

THE CONCEPT OF REVOLUTION
Revolution as Imperative

As WE arrive at the exposition of the main theme of Bakunin's anarchist creed, the problem of revolution, we must again remember his inconsistency. Although at this point the inconsistency is less obvious than elsewhere in Bakunin's reasoning, there is still enough to be an obstacle to the correct comprehension of his concept. If all of Bakunin's pronouncements on the subject of revolution are treated on the same level, the picture is rather obscure. Thus, although in Bakunin's view revolution is the highest ideal, we may find statements to the effect that revolution is a "social stupidity."[1] Or we may be told that the anarchist "revolution will not enrage men against men," but on the next page we find the statement that "one should scarcely be astonished if, in the first moment [of revolution], the outraged people kill many."[2] On another occasion, Bakunin frankly admits that "revolution means war, and this implies the destruction of men and things."[3]

However, this inconsistency is more apparent than real, and much of the contradiction disappears when we succeed in establishing the motives for Bakunin's controversial statements. Bakunin's renunciations of revolution were hardly dictated by momentary doubts as to the expediency of revolution. As a rule, they had tactical causes. In order to clear up the inconsistencies, we must distinguish between what Bakunin considered as principles and what as tactics. With regard to principles, Bakunin was unshakeable, but in respect to tactics, extremely flexible. He repeatedly underlined the importance of tactics:

Remember, my dear friends, and keep repeating to yourselves a hundred, a thousand times a day, that upon

[1] Bakunin, *Complete Collection*, I, 233.
[2] Bakunin, *Gesammelte Werke*, III, 87, 86.
[3] Bakunin, *Works, Golos Truda* ed., III, 12.

the establishment of this line of conduct depends the outcome of revolution: victory or defeat.[4]

It is necessary to keep this peculiarity of Bakunin's reasoning
in mind when evaluating his concept of revolution.

Bakunin was one of those radicals who reach the conclusion
that revolution is necessary, regardless of the point of the critique
of society from which they start. And since the theories which
he made use of permitted the construction of something like
a system of revolutionism, Bakunin was able to make its conceptual construction. In both his reasoning and his action, the
élan of revolution reached its zenith. He was, as Sombart says,
the man who combined all the attributes necessary for becoming
the father of modern revolutionism.[5] Therefore, his influence
was not limited to the anarchist movement; it also left its mark,
direct or indirect, on the whole revolutionary movement of
Europe, especially that of the Bolsheviks.

Bakunin frequently attempted to give a philosophical foundation to revolution. The whole history of mankind appears to
him as:

> . . . the revolutionary negation of the past . . . . Man has
> liberated himself (by breaking the divine commandment
> not to eat of the tree of knowledge), he has divided him-
> self from animal nature and made himself man; he began
> his history and his human development with his act of
> disobedience and knowledge, i.e., with rebellion and
> thought.[6]

Bakunin maintained that there were three principles which
were the driving force of both the individual and the historical
process. These are human animality, thought, and revolt. Social
and private economy correspond to the first, science to the
second, and freedom to the third. According to Bakunin,
the human being has an innate need for revolt, a revolutionary
instinct.[7] Therefore, man's perpetual rebellion, which may lead
him to self-sacrifice and self-destruction, does not depend on
either right or obligation but is immediately bestowed along
with his humanity. Since spiritual emancipation presupposes
thought, history is meaningful only as a history of perpetual
revolution. In this sense, revolution ceases to be a particular

[4] *Ibid.*, IV, 179.
[5] W. Sombart, *Der proletarische Sozialismus* (Jena, 1924), I, 179.
[6] Bakunin, *Gesammelte Werke*, I, 96, 102.
[7] *Ibid.*, p. 96.

historical phase in the human process, and becomes a category of the human spirit. No longer is it what it had originally been, an unavoidable means to a rationally established end; it is an end in itself. Revolution is considered either as a theoretically perpetual situation, or as a practically almost infinite process. In theory, it may at some time cease and be replaced by a new order; in practice, it lasts so long that it must claim the attention of at least a whole generation. Long before the March Revolution, Bakunin stated that the task of his generation was to destroy, and that the building would be done by others who would be better, wiser and fresher.[8] He never abandoned this view. According to this approach, revolution is an accelerated but perpetual process of adaptation of the forms of social life to its essence. In this, there is nothing of an anarchist nature other than the belief that it will be perpetual. The anarchist discrepancy lies in the idea that the torpid law, state, and other social institutions are not to be replaced by newer, more suitable ones, but are to be eliminated completely and forever. This is probably the final *contradictio in adjecto* of the anarchist creed. It demands the expressions of life, but it insists that these shall not be vested in any forms, or at least that these forms shall not have any influence on content.

This left Bakunin with no alternative but to declare that the will to destroy is at the same time a creative will. The consequence of this attitude was the belief that revolution took on the dimensions of an apocalyptic catastrophe of the old world, "the social revolution, which the imagination of the West, tempered as it is by civilization, can hardly imagine."[9] Therefore, Bakunin equated revolution to the unchaining of what is called "evil passions," and the destruction of what is called "public order."[10] This negative passion does not rise to the great height of the revolutionary cause, but without that passion, the revolution cannot be achieved, for there can be no revolution "without a sweeping and passionate destruction, a salutary and fruitful destruction, since by means of such destruction new worlds are born and come into existence."[11]

Hence, revolution should not "leave one stone upon another, over the entire earth."[12] In a word, revolution is equivalent to pan-destruction.

[8] Polonski, *Materialy*, I, 177.   [9] Bakunin, *Gesammelte Werke*, II, 54.
[10] *Ibid.*, III, 87.   [11] Maximoff, *op. cit.*, p. 381.
[12] Bakunin, *Gesammelte Werke*, III, 85.

This approach of Bakunin had as a corollary his belief that any non-revolutionary political action was meaningless or even harmful. This led Bakunin to advocate "apolitism," rejection of political action by the working class within the framework of the existing political order. "Apolitism" was the ideological basis of Bakunin's clash with Marx in the International. Bakunin said: "Nothing has had a more harmful influence on the workers than has bourgeois political liberty."[13]

Bakunin's arguments on this point were parallel to those of the later syndicalists. They proceeded from the assumption that "the state, however popular it may be made in form, will always be an institution of domination and exploitation."[14] In other words, the state is always merely an instrument of the capitalist ruling class. The workers cannot make use of political democracy because they "lack the material means which are necessary to make political liberty a reality" and because their education and knowledge of affairs are insufficient. And once a worker is elected to parliament, he becomes part and parcel of the state, corrupted by bourgeois parliamentarianism, "ceasing in fact to be a worker and becoming a statesman instead."[15] For this reason, parliamentary bodies are meaningless, because the representative system rests upon a fiction, and universal suffrage is an artificial device.[16]

> One must be a donkey, ignorant, crazy, to hope that any constitution, even the most liberal, most democratic one, can improve the relationship of the state to the people.[17]

In this way, Bakunin rejected the basic premises of parliamentary democracy and advocated only action which would undermine the very fundamentals of contemporary society. Such a way is the more promising, according to Bakunin, because after its first stages, capitalist society produces a decadent cowardly bourgeoisie without faith in the future.[18] "It is the 'barbarians' (the proletariat) who now represent faith in human destiny and in the future of civilization."[19] It is the task of the

---

[13] M. A. Bakunin, *Vsesvetnyi revolutsionnyi soyuz sotsiyalnoi demokratii* (Berlin, 1904), p. 51.
[14] Bakunin, *Works*, Golos Truda ed., V, 20.
[15] Bakunin, *Selected Works*, p. 268.
[16] Bakunin, *Works*, Golos Truda ed., II, 30ff.
[17] *Ibid.*, I, 109.   [18] Bakunin, *Gesammelte Werke*, II, 243.
[19] Bakunin, *Works*, Golos Truda ed., V, 37.

actively organized minority to exploit these latent instincts of the masses.

In moments of great political and economic crisis, when the instincts of the masses are sharpened to the utmost keenness and are open to all worth-while suggestions, at a time when these herds of human slaves, crushed and enslaved but still unresigned, rise up at last to throw off their yoke, but feeling bewildered and powerless because of being completely disorganized—then ten, twenty or thirty well organized persons, acting in concert and knowing where they are going and what they want, can easily carry along one, two or three hundred people, or even more.[20]

Bakunin rejected the idea of forming legal political parties representing the interests of the workers. The labor coöperative movement, in his opinion, could only produce "a new collectivist bourgeoisie," and "truly socialist coöperation, the coöperation of the future, is virtually unattainable at present."[21] Bakunin's attitude toward trade unions was different, but on the whole, he paid only superficial attention to this question. In one of his occasional pronouncements on trade unions, he stated that he saw:

. . . in the organization of the trade unions, their federation in the International, and their representation by the Chambers of Labor . . . the living germs of the new social order which is to replace the bourgeois world.[22]

Thus, according to Bakunin, trade unions were "creating not only the ideas but also the facts of the future itself."[23] But on the whole, he considered trade unions as insufficient in themselves to be a tool for social transformation.

Strikes were favored by Bakunin, because they trained the workers for the ultimate struggle. He recommended them for the following reasons.

Strikes awaken in the masses all the social-revolutionary instincts . . . . Every strike is more valuable in that it broadens and deepens to an ever greater extent the gulf now separating the bourgeois class from the masses of the people. Strikes . . . destroy . . . the possibility of any compromise or deal with the enemy. When

[20] *Ibid.*, V, 50.　　　　　　　　　　[21] *Ibid.*, V, 24.
[22] Quoted in Kenafick, *op. cit.*, p. 257.　　[23] *Ibid.*

strikes begin to grow in scope and intensity, spreading from one place to another, it means that events are ripening for a general strike, and a general strike coming off at the present time, now that the proletariat is deeply permeated with the ideas of emancipation, can only lead to a great cataclysm, which will regenerate society.[24]

The resemblance of these ideas of Bakunin's to those of the later syndicalists is obvious. There were, however, many reasons for the fact that Bakunin never renounced his revolution in favor of a general strike. The first was that he could not expect a general strike to accomplish the pan-destruction which he considered as the first condition for successful social transformation. A second reason was that, according to Bakunin, "only a sweeping revolution, embracing both the city workers and the peasants, would be sufficiently strong to overthrow and break the organized power of the state."[25] Bakunin was fully aware of the complete unfitness of the peasantry for a general strike, and this argument had the more force since that stratum of society overwhelmingly outnumbered any other in Russian society. Russia was always within the orbit of Bakunin's interest, despite his close connection with and participation in the revolutionary movement of western Europe. Therefore, in Bakunin's schemes, revolution always retained an unshakeable position, and the general strike was relegated to the remote background. In this also, Bakunin's pattern was close to that of the Bolsheviks.

In regard to the preconditions for revolution, Bakunin once stated:

Revolutions are not improvised. They are not made at will by individuals. They come about through the force of circumstances, and are independent of any deliberate will or conspiracy. They can be foreseen, but their explosion can never be accelerated.[26]

Since, as we have seen, one side of Bakunin's analysis of contemporary reality was based on Marxism, this statement might lead us to believe that Bakunin applied deterministic laws to the question of the coming of revolution and did not leave any space for free human action and choice.

Such a view could, however, be completely inadequate, for

[24] Maximoff, *op. cit.*, pp. 384, 383; Bakunin, *Gesammelte Werke*, II, 50-51.
[25] Bakunin, *Works, Golos Truda* ed., IV, 213.
[26] *Ibid.*, IV, 21.

it is refuted by Bakunin's actions and by other of his writings. But while the example of Bakunin's life gives the impression that he believed that a revolution might be started at almost any given historical moment, his writings show that this also is an incomplete expression. In his writings we see that the coming of a revolution is conditioned by many factors and that only a conjunction of all of them can produce a revolution and safeguard its success.

Poverty, for instance, although it engenders a revolutionary instinct, is by no means sufficient to produce revolution. Even when poverty drives man to the extremes of despair, the indignation which it arouses may only provoke a limited number of local revolts, inadequate to arouse the masses of the people to a universal, decisive revolution.[27]

Nor, as Bakunin repeated many times, can revolution be imposed "by decrees." By this, he meant the capture of the central power of the state by a revolutionary party or secret organization, in a *coup d'état,* while the broad masses of the population remain passive. Bakunin rejected such methods for achieving social transformation as doomed to fail. He always combined his rejections with vitriolic attacks against the "revolutionary Jacobins" and the "socialists of the school of Blanqui,"[28] to whom he attributed such ideas and plots.

Thus, in Bakunin's eyes, neither socio-economic conditions nor capture of state power by the revolutionaries was sufficient to produce a revolution. He allotted the decisive role to the revolutionary ideal. To the socio-economic factors, a psychological one, that of revolutionary consciousness, had to be added. Only thus could the preconditions for revolution be supplied. He wrote:

> . . . that [revolution] can take place only when the people are stirred by a universal idea, one evolved historically from the depths of popular instinct, and developed, broadened and clarified by a series of significant events and distressing and bitter experiences. It can take place only when the people in general have an idea of their rights and a deep, passionate, one might almost say religious, faith in those rights. When this ideal and this power and this popular faith meet poverty of the sort which drives man to desperation, then the social revolu-

[27] *Ibid.,* I, 76.   [28] *Ibid.,* IV, 175.

tion is near and inevitable, and no power in the world would be able to stop it.[29]

Hence, the essence of Bakunin's preconditions for revolution are the political and psychological maturity of the people, emergent revolutionary consciousness. In contrast with Marx's doctrine of the economic causality of revolution, Bakunin's principles are psychological. This allowed a large degree of flexibility in predicting the outbreak of revolution. It left free space for human choice and action. Therefore, in Bakunin's doctrine, unlike Marx's, the economic backwardness of a country was not an obstacle to revolution. Since the decisive factor was ideological, even an economically advanced country might be backward in regard to revolutionary potential.

> The reasoning of Marx leads to an absolutely contrary opinion. Taking into consideration only the economic question, he says that the most advanced countries, and consequently those the most capable of making a social revolution, are those in which modern capitalist production has reached its highest level of development.[30]

For these reasons, Bakunin's estimate of the revolutionary ripeness of the various countries of his time disregarded their industrial advancement. He selected Russia, Spain, and Italy as the countries closest to revolution. And, after the March Revolution, he abandoned hope of revolution in Germany, although that country was then making great industrial progress. Bakunin expected that the revolution would probably, though not necessarily, start in western Europe. He also stated: "If the workers in the West linger too long, the Russian peasants will outstrip them by their own example."[31]

Bakunin's views about the conditions necessary for revolution remove him from the theoretical premises of *putschism*. However, he also upheld the thesis that "each rebellion, no matter how unsuccessful, is useful."[32] Although the justification for this attitude deviates from the principles of *putschism* (Bakunin considered unsuccessful uprisings as useful in accelerating the ripening of revolutionary consciousness), the final practical effects are very similar.

In order to be successful, a revolution must not only have the preconditions outlined, it must also be waged at a suitable

[29] *Ibid.*, I, 76-77.   [30] Bakunin, *Gesammelte Werke*, III, 245.
[31] *Ibid.*, III, 131.   [32] Bakunin, *Complete Collection*, II, 260.

moment. In fixing this moment, Bakunin's opinions evolved, and in his last years he saw it in time of war, finally in the world war.[33] Bakunin believed that war should be converted into civil war in the countries involved. This is the main theme of his book, as usual unfinished, *The Knouto-Germanic Empire and the Social Revolution.* In this, he laid exceptional stress on the expediency of such a method.

It is not difficult to see the resemblance, with regard to the preconditions for revolution, between the views of Bakunin and those of the Bolsheviks. Indeed, this similarity is obvious. It cannot be denied that there is truth in Cunow's remarks: "The theory of Bolshevism, or rather of Leninism, is nothing other than a relapse into Bakuninism, into certain doctrines of Michael Bakunin."[34] Cunow came to this conclusion on the basis of a rather superficial acquaintance with Bakunin's teaching. However, a more profound study of Bakunin's concept of revolution only reinforces such a view, adducing a number of convincing arguments on its behalf.

Revolutionary Forces

The next question to arise is that of the forces to carry out revolution, that of the social strata on which it should rest. Here again, Bakunin's answer was complex, even more elaborate than that to the question of the preconditions for revolution. This was because of the fact that the revolution which Bakunin proposed had many aims.

Since the revolution was to abolish exploitation, this automatically made it the task of the exploited, i.e., in Bakunin's view, of the workers and peasants. On this presumption, it was the duty of the working masses to emancipate themselves. Since revolution should make an end to exploitation and should bring the emancipation of the exploited, it must be "social." Only such a revolution, in Bakunin's opinion, justifies the effort needed to make it.

Bakunin's revolution was also to have been "universal." "No revolution can count on success unless it spreads speedily beyond the individual nation to all other nations."[35] In Bakunin's scheme, a revolution, to be successful, had to be a world revo-

[33] Bakunin, *Gesammelte Werke,* III, 273.
[34] H. Cunow, *Die Marxsche Geschichts-, Gesellschafts- und Staatslehre* (Berlin, Vol. I, 1920; Vol. II, 1921), I, 335.
[35] Bakunin, *Gesammelte Werke,* III, 85.

lution, or at least an all-European one in its first stage. This led
to another specification. In the West, he considered the proletariat to be the chief revolutionary force, and although he considered the participation of the peasantry to be indispensable
even here, he placed it in a secondary position. But in eastern
Europe, and particularly in Russia, where the proletarian stratum
was largely lacking in his time, he made the peasantry the chief
revolutionary force. This, of course, inevitably had a decisive
influence on the very character and course of his revolution.
Therefore, the revolution which he schemed for the East, for
Russia, approached in appearance a blind, instinctive rebellion
of the outraged peasants. And yet Bakunin's Russian background and preoccupation with the possibilities of revolution in
Russia led him to introduce many such elements into his schemes
for revolution in western Europe also.

The revolution which Bakunin proposed also aimed at frantic
pan-destruction. From this nihilistic aspect, it would have been
the equivalent of the negation and annihilation of contemporary
civilization. This induced him to scrutinize revolutionary forces
according to another criterion, that of "barbarism." This was
the source of his continual references to the men who have
"Satan in the flesh," or who happily preserve "barbarism." He
assured himself, and tried to convince others, that this indispensable revolutionary quality was fully possessed by the
workers, and especially by the peasants. He stated: ". . . these
[West European] workers and peasants still have a full future
and constitute a 'barbarism' which will, in its own good time,
renew the West."[36]

It seems, however, that he may have had some doubts as
to the latent existence of "barbarism" among the mass of the
peasants and workers, for he sought social elements possessing
this "virtue" more fully. He put extraordinary emphasis on the
necessity of their participation in the revolution. It was the
déclassés whom he found to be most apt.

Bakunin elaborated the specifications for this social stratum,
and even included criminals and brigands and the like as potential revolutionaries, at least for Russia.

> There is someone in Russian society who has the
> courage to march against the world; this is the brigand.

[36] Quoted in Kenafick, *op. cit.*, p. 171.

The first rebels, the first revolutionaries in Russia, Puga-
chev and Stenka Razin, were brigands.[37]

Now we ask which of these social strata or social splinter
groups were, in Bakunin's opinion, called to carry out the revolution. His answer was all of them; only the combined action
of all of these social elements could wage successful revolution;
all had to be yoked together to make it.

Bakunin did not believe, however, that they could harness
themselves together instinctively, without outside help. Although
he always said that: "The spontaneous action of the masses
should be everything,"[38] he simultaneously admitted that:
"Against this terrible argument [the military and police force of
the state], which the workers will oppose not with intelligence,
organization or collective will, but with the sheer will power of
their despair, the proletariat will be more impotent than before."[39] Therefore, it is necessary "to organize the popular
forces to carry out the revolution . . . this is the only task of
those who sincerely aim at its emancipation."[40] Bakunin clearly
stated that "an elemental force lacking organization is not a
real power."[41]

Therefore, Bakunin found another element to be needed, one
crowning all the others. The previously mentioned ones were to
provide only the revolutionary fuel, more or less consciously.
A conductor was still needed. This was to be the secret revolutionary organization. Bakunin explained:

> However, for the victory of the revolution over re-
> action, it is necessary that in the midst of the people's
> anarchy, which is the very life and the entire energy of
> the revolution, the unity of revolutionary thought and
> action find an organ. This organ must be the secret and
> universal association . . . .[42]

This secret organization was to be neither "a theoretic or
exclusively economic organization" (an allusion to the trade
unions, etc.), not an "academy or workshop," but a "militant
association" of professional revolutionaries.[43] For membership
in the secret organization, class background was irrelevant,
passionate devotion to the revolutionary cause everything. "Bar-

[37] Bakunin, *Complete Collection*, II, 256.
[38] Bakunin, *Works, Golos Truda* ed., IV, 257.
[39] *Ibid.*, IV, 219-220.   [40] *Ibid.*, I, 91.   [41] Maximoff, *op. cit.*, p. 367.
[42] Bakunin, *Gesammelte Werke*, III, 96.   [43] *Ibid.*, III, 109.

barism" was of no avail, instead the members were to have "a devil in the flesh." This secret organization was to have charge of the final, essential polishing of preparatory revolutionary action. It would "act as midwife at the birth of the revolution."[44] And after the outbreak of revolution, this organization was to have exclusive responsibility for its course by "mediating between revolutionary thought and the instincts of the masses."[45] The secret society was to be the revolution's "invisible pilot, not through any visible power, but as the collective dictatorship of all the Allies [the name of the members of the conspiratory society], a dictatorship without any badge, without title, without official right, and the more powerful because it lacks the appearance of power." Bakunin concluded: "This is the only dictatorship which I can concede."[46]

In this way, the cause of revolution was gradually shifted to become primarily the affair of the secret society. The masses of the people, in return for promises of a splendid future, were to become the unconscious tool of the invisible society which was conscious indeed of its aim. And it was in the creation of such a society that Bakunin saw his own main task. In a letter, he stated:

> . . . all my ambition . . . is directed . . . toward helping you to create that invisible collective power which alone can save and direct the revolution.[47]

In summary, we must remember that Bakunin considered all of the social strata mentioned, plus the secret organization of revolutionaries, as indispensable to a successful revolution. No one of them, acting separately, was sufficient. This must be kept in mind as we proceed to more detailed remarks about the composition of revolutionary forces in Bakunin's schemes.

In general, Bakunin's reliance on the workers as a potential revolutionary force went along with the common line of contemporary socialist thought, and therefore, it is unnecessary to go into this point. What was his own idea was that of crediting them with the quality of "barbarism," indispensable to and interchangeable with revolutionism. Thus, he gave assurance that:

It is the "barbarians" (the proletariat) who now

[44] *Ibid.*, III, 90.   [45] *Ibid.*
[46] *Ibid.*, III, 98-99.   [47] *Ibid.*

represent faith in human destiny and in the future of civilization, and the "civilized" may now expect their salvation only from barbarism.[48]

Bakunin's particular contribution was his advocacy of the peasants as a potential revolutionary element. He took great pains to explain this and to try to popularize this view. It was his opinion that:

> An uprising by the proletariat alone would not be enough; with that we would have only a political revolution which would necessarily produce a natural and legitimate reaction on the part of the peasants. That reaction, or even the mere indifference of the peasants, would strangle the revolution of the cities . . . .

Therefore, says Bakunin:

> Only a sweeping revolution, embracing both the urban workers and the peasants, would be sufficiently strong to overthrow and break the organized power of the state.[49]

Bakunin's basic view with regard to the peasants, at least those of western Europe, was that "the peasants in the country create the army of reaction today. However, the peasants can and must be converted to the cause of revolution."[50]

> [The peasants] can be stirred into action, and sooner or later they will be stirred by the social revolution. This is true for three reasons: a) Owing to their backward or relatively *barbarous* civilization, they have retained in all integrity the simple robust temperament and the energy germane to the folk nature. b) They live from the labor of their hands, and are morally conditioned by this labor, which fosters an instinctive hatred for all the privileged parasites of the state, and for all the exploiters of labor. c) Finally, being toilers themselves, they share common interests with the city workers, from whom they are separated by their prejudices.[51]

Yet, according to Bakunin, the vital factor in the peasants' potential revolutionism is the fact that they do not feel a need for the existence of the state. "Peasants hate all governments," says Bakunin, "and only tolerate them from slyness."[52] For them,

---

[48] Bakunin, *Works, Golos Truda* ed., V, 37.
[49] *Ibid.*, V, 202.
[50] Bakunin, *Gesammelte Werke*, II, 253.
[51] *Bakunin, Works, Golos Truda* ed., IV, 212.
[52] Bakunin, *Gesammelte Werke*, I, 26.

a state is only a collector of taxes. One should not be misled by the fact that peasants are often supporters of the monarch. Such support is only apparent, arising from the peasants' illusion that the monarch is their defender against the landlords. Since revolution would eliminate the landlords, the source of the peasants' favorable disposition toward the monarch would disappear.[53]

Neither is the religious bigotry of the peasants an insurmountable obstacle. It may be overcome by suitable tactics, by:

> . . . so arranging that the interests of the peasants will inevitably clash with the interests of the church. After 1789 their religious superstition did not prevent them from buying the properties of the church which had been confiscated by the state.[54]

Therefore, this is a starting point for including the peasants in the revolution.

> [The peasants] hate the essence of the state in so far as they come in touch with it, and are always ready to destroy it, in so far as they are not restrained by the organized force of government.[55]

These were the principles of Bakunin's approach to the peasantry. But the tactics were to be extremely flexible and cautious. Bakunin tirelessly repeated that it was essential to use suitable means in the rousing of the peasants to revolutionary uprising.[56]

His view was that the anti-state feelings of the peasants could and must be mobilized by direct appeal to their economic and class instincts. "They must be offered and immediately given great material advantages."[57]

> Since the peasants love land, they should be allowed to seize the land and drive out the landlords and all those who exploit the labor of others. They are reluctant to pay mortgages and taxes, so let them stop paying. Let those among them who do not want to pay their private debts be freed from the necessity of paying such debts. And finally, since the peasants detest conscription, let them be freed from duty of furnishing soldiers to the army.[58]

[53] Bakunin, *Works, Golos Truda* ed., V, 178.
[54] *Ibid.*, IV, 174-175.   [55] Maximoff, *op. cit.*, p. 364.
[56] Bakunin, *Works, Golos Truda* ed., IV, 178.
[57] Bakunin, *Gesammelte Werke*, I, 28.
[58] Bakunin, *Works, Golos Truda* ed., IV, 187.

Therefore, Bakunin felt that the anti-state feelings of the peasants, or rather their indifference toward the state, might be harnessed to the revolutionary cause by drawing for them a rosy prospect of material advantages, particularly by allowing and encouraging them to seize the land. He believed that it would be relatively easy to mobilize the peasants where they were hungry for land but was rather pessimistic about the possibility of including the peasants in revolutionary projects where their economic situation was different.

On this basis, Bakunin relied on the peasantry of Russia and saw it as the main revolutionary driving force there. He also considered the Italian and Spanish peasants as reliable revolutionary elements:

> The peasants in the great part of Italy are miserably poor, much poorer than the workers in the cities. They are not proprietors like the peasants in France, which fact is of course highly fortunate from the point of view of the revolution.[59]

Because of the different situation of the French peasants, Bakunin was somewhat uneasy about them, though he still hoped for their participation in the revolution. He said: "The French peasant is greedy . . . ."[60] He also made the following reminder:

> One should not forget that the peasants of France, certainly a vast majority of them, although owning their lands, nevertheless live by their own labor. This is what separates them essentially from the bourgeois class . . . .[61]

Bakunin was not hopeful about the peasants in cases where there was no place for an immediate exhortation to seize the landlords' lands. Here, his reliance on the peasants' admirable "barbarism" and toiling way of life was of little or no value. For instance, he wrote the following about the German peasantry:

> . . . in Germany there was [before the March Revolution] an element which does not exist today, i.e. a revolutionary peasantry, or at least one capable of being made revolutionary. At that time there were still vestiges of

---

[59] Maximoff, *op. cit.*, p. 205.
[60] Bakunin, *Gesammelte Werke*, I, 34.
[61] Maximoff, *op. cit.*, p. 205.

serfdom, as there are still in the Duchies of Mecklem-
burg. In Austria the law of serfdom still reigned completely. There was no doubt that the German peasants
were fitted and ready for uprising.[62]

While advocating that in the revolution the peasants should
seize the landlords' estates, he admonished against any expropriation of the lands of the peasants. Impetuously, as usual,
he warned against such a step by affirming:

> If after the proclamation of social liquidation an
> attempt were to be made to expropriate by decree the
> millions of these small farmers, this would inevitably throw
> them back into the camp of reaction.[63]

But this put Bakunin into a predicament with his own demand for the abolition of all private property and for the establishment of collective ownership (including that of land). It
also led to objections by his opponents that peasants are by
nature proprietors and that their partition of the estates would
result in strengthening the social stratum of small landholders.
Bakunin's resolution of this contradiction can only be called a
trick, or a socio-political deception on a large scale, although
it is another question whether or not his device was practicable.

Zealously, Bakunin advocated the abolition of the law of
inheritance; this was the main subject of dispute between his
followers and those of Marx at the Basel Congress of the International.[64] The idea that laws of inheritance should be done
away with was widespread in the socialist movement of the
time, as a means of leveling social discrepancies. Its growing
popularity may be traced to the Saint-Simonian school.[65] But
Bakunin assigned to it, beside this main task, an additional
one—a tactical role. The abolition of inheritance was to be a
less drastic means to substitute for the expropriation of the
small landholders. Capitalist ownership was to be abolished
immediately by the revolution, but not that of the small owners:

> If you proclaim the political and juridical liquidation
> of the state simultaneously with the social liquidation,
> if you abolish the law of inheritance, then what will re-
> main to the peasants? Only bare factual possession;
> this possession, lacking any legal sanction, without the

---

[62] Bakunin, *Works, Golos Truda* ed., 1, 201.
[63] Quoted in Steklov, *op. cit.*, III, 373.
[64] Carr, *op. cit.*, pp. 364ff.   [65] Gray, *op. cit.*, p. 165.

mighty support of the state, will easily be changed under
the pressure of revolutionary events and forces.[66]

But, since Bakunin's revolution was to do away with the
institution of the state completely, was not his strong emphasis
on the law of inheritance somewhat illogical? He tried to clear
up this inconsistency, saying that the law of inheritance would
disappear:

> . . . inasmuch as the state and the whole juridical insti-
> tution, the defense of property by the state, and family
> right, including the law of inheritance, necessarily will
> disappear in the terrific whirlwind of revolutionary
> anarchy. There will be no more political or juridical
> right—there will be only revolutionary facts . . . Property
> will cease to be a right and will be reduced to the status
> of a simple fact.[67]

To the objection of his opponents that such a method would
lead to civil war, Bakunin answered that this was so much the
better, saying: "Why do you fear it so much?" He continued
with the assurance:

> And do not believe that if these arrangements are
> concluded apart from the tutelage of any official author-
> ity, but are brought about by the force of circumstance,
> the stronger and wealthier peasants will exercise a pre-
> dominant influence. Once the wealth of the rich has lost
> the guarantee of the laws, it will cease to be a power . . . .
> As for the more cunning and the economically stronger
> peasants, they will have to yield to the collective power
> of the peasant mass, to the great number of poor and very
> poor peasants, as well as to the rural proletarians.

Bakunin concluded:

> But what is to prevent the weaker elements from uniting
> in order to plunder the stronger?[68]

After establishing, by these arguments, that it was necessary
to draw the peasants into participation in a revolution, Bakunin
did not, however, allot to them the leading role. The leading
role (though not the leadership, which was reserved for the
secret society of professional revolutionaries) was, according

[66] Quoted in Steklov, *op. cit.*, III, 373.
[67] Bakunin, *Works, Golos Truda* ed., IV, 187; Bakunin, *Gesammelte Werke*,
I, 34.
[68] Bakunin, *Works, Golos Truda* ed., IV, 187-189.

to Bakunin, to be taken by the proletariat in western Europe, and in Russia, where a proletariat was lacking, by the intelligentsia. He stated:

> In order that the peasants may rise in rebellion, it is absolutely necessary that the city workers take upon themselves the initiative in this revolutionary movement, because it is only the city workers who today combine in themselves the instinct, the clear consciousness, the idea and the conscious will of the Socialist Revolution.[69]

Therefore:

> In the interests of the revolution the workers should stop flaunting their disdain for the peasants. Faced by the bourgeois exploiter, the worker should feel that he is the brother of the peasant.[70]

Repeating his *ceterum censeo*, Bakunin concluded:

> Only a wide-sweeping revolution, embracing both the city workers and the peasants, will be sufficiently strong to overthrow and break the organized power of the state.[71]

Taking all of these elements of Bakunin's revolutionary pattern for the peasants together, one can hardly fail to compare them with those of the Bolshevik plan. There is a striking similarity with the Bolshevik slogans to "take over all the land," with simultaneous nationalization of the land, with the Bolshevik method of "carrying class war into the villages," and with the emphasis on the leading role of the city proletariat to the revolutionary peasantry. The deviations which appear are of a rather secondary nature. They are caused by the practical difficulties which arose in carrying out the accepted postulates. But, by and large, the core of the Bolsheviks' revolutionary policy toward the peasantry coincides with that proposed by Bakunin. In regard to this similarity, Steklov, at one time the chief Soviet scholar of Bakunin and himself an eminent Bolshevik partisan, who submitted revolutionary schemes toward the peasantry to only a partial discussion in his biography of Bakunin, made the following remark:

> In this sense one must say that Bakunin was one of the first to put the issue of drawing the peasants into the socialist movement into a more or less concrete form.

Steklov says further:

[69] *Ibid.*, IV, 213.   [70] *Ibid.*, IV, 183.   [71] *Ibid.*, V, 202.

All that Bakunin had to say about the necessity of creating solidarity between the workers and the peasants against the exploiters, and about the means to be used to attract the peasants to the side of the social revolution (primarily the expropriation of the great landowners and transferral of the land to the peasants) makes him kin to contemporary Communism and also to the Soviet Republic, which in this field has employed a policy quite similar to that proposed by Bakunin.[72]

In connection with the problem of revolutionary forces, Bakunin's attention also turned to those splinter social groups of contemporary society who might be called by the general term of *déclassés,* though not always necessarily in the negative coloring of this word. He assigned an important revolutionary role to them, searched them out with great care, and greeted happily every manifestation of their existence. Here again, as with the workers and the peasants, his view differed, depending on whether he was dealing with western Europe or with Russia.

In western Europe, he found such an element primarily in the *Lumpenproletariat.*

In Italy there exists a huge group, by nature extremely wise although mostly illiterate, the wretchedly poor proletariat. This consists of two or three millions of city and factory workers and small artisans and about twenty million peasant non-proprietors . . . . Probably nowhere is the social revolution so near as in Italy. In Italy there does not exist, as there does in many European countries, a settled working stratum, partially privileged because of its considerable earnings, even boasting of some literary education and moreover impregnated by bourgeois principles, strivings and vanity, and considering that although belonging to the working people, it differs from the bourgeoisie only in factual situation and not in aims. In Germany and Switzerland especially there are many such workers. In Italy, on the contrary, there are few, so few that they vanish in the mass and are without any importance and influence. In Italy there prevails the wretchedly poor proletariat, about which Messers. Marx and Engels, and following them the whole German Social Democratic school, speak with such deep disdain. Surely this is a mistake, since it is in this proletariat, and only

72 Steklov, *op. cit.,* III, 282.

in this, not in the bourgeois rank of the working class, that the whole reason and strength of the future Social Revolution lie.[73]

Yet, Bakunin uses the terms "proletariat" and "working class" as often as "the masses of ordinary laborers" or the "stratum of ordinary laborers" or the "ordinary working people." It would appear that by such expressions he means the stratum described in this passage. In his scheme of the revolutionary forces, the emphasis clearly is shifted from the working class as a whole to the stratum which may be called the *Lumpenproletariat.*

Bakunin found a revolutionary element of the same sort in the *déclassé* bourgeois youth. He wrote:

. . . Italy and Spain are perhaps the most revolutionary countries. In Italy there exists something that is lacking in other countries: a vehement, energetic youth, upset from its social position, without the prospect of a career, without an exit, which, despite its bourgeois origin, is not morally and intellectually exhausted, like the youth of the other bourgeois countries.[74]

Bakunin called the people of bourgeois origin who fully identified themselves with the working masses "a real treasure," since, in his view, they:

. . . bring to the people the essential knowledge, the ability to generalize facts, the skill needed to organize, to create associations. This produces the conscious fighting force without which victory is unthinkable.[75]

Bakunin was not even disposed to disdain those elements which approached the criminal and frequently occupied himself with the idea of including them in the revolution he proposed.

In Berlin there was to be found [during the March Revolution] even that element which up to now has been famous only in Paris: the tough—a crook and revolutionary hero at the same time.[76]

In Russia, since the industrial working class was only beginning to emerge, Bakunin laid all his hopes of revolutionizing the country on the intelligentsia. In his time, the formation of this new stratum of Russian society was proceeding rapidly,

---

[73] Bakunin, *Works, Golos Truda* ed., I, 49-51.
[74] Bakunin, *Gesammelte Werke*, III, 120, 121.
[75] Bakunin, *Works, Golos Truda* ed., I, 49.
[76] *Ibid.*, I, 200.

and in a relatively short time it emerged as a distinct and weighty social class. The Russian term for it *raznochintzy* (people of various positions), is a clear indication of its social origin. This class was formed from various splinters of Russian society, united by the possession of education (though of very different degrees of education—it included even the village teacher) and by the spirit of social idealism, the passion for improving the world, disrespect for all tradition, and by a tense, disinterested enthusiasm. This Russian social stratum had no real counterpart in western Europe, and the term "intelligentsia" is by no means to be taken as a synonym for "intellectuals."

It was this new social formation which Bakunin expected to revolutionize Russia. About this group he wrote:

> In Russia there exists the second element of power [the first was the peasants, the "people"]; one which is not stratified because it is established upon the rejection of any stratification. It is composed of innumerable persons of all strata: gentry, civil servants, clergy, merchants, townspeople and peasants. And not only in its spirit and thought, but often in its very way of life it is in contradiction to the existing reality of Russia, it is ready to give up its life for the future, and it lives only by its reliance on the future. It creates, we might say, a homeless wandering church of freedom.

This group "engenders deeds and awakens the peoples."[77]

These are Bakunin's expressions in his later years, but they do not differ from his earlier prognoses. Even before the March Revolution, when the formation of this class of intelligentsia was beginning, he made the following characterization in a speech on the occasion of the anniversary of the insurrection of Poland:

> . . . a marginal class, sufficiently numerous, and composed of very various elements, restless, fierce—a class which will throw itself into the first revolutionary movement.[78]

Here again, as in Italy, Bakunin saw the youth as the most promising element of the whole Russian intelligentsia.

The world of educated, reckless youngsters, not finding

[77] Quoted in Steklov, *op. cit.*, II, 28-29.
[78] Bakunin, *Selected Works*, p. 10. Speaking of this statement, which Bakunin made in 1847, Steklov says that he was a prophet (Steklov, *op. cit.*, II, 29).

for themselves a place or an opportunity for occupation in Russia, this is the phalanx of thousands which, consciously or unconsciously, belongs to the revolution.[79]

In regard to Russia, Bakunin stressed especially the need to include criminal elements in the making of a revolution. He was thinking of the Russian brigands, the element in Russian society with the "courage to march against the world."[80]

> Therefore, in getting close to the people, we [revolutionaries] must first of all join those elements of the masses which, ever since the foundation of the state power of Moscow, have never ceased to protest, not only in words but also in deeds, against everything which is connected with the state, directly or indirectly . . . . Let us join with the bold world of bandits, the only genuine revolutionists in Russia.[81]

Thus, Bakunin considered that every element which was in conflict with the existing order, for whatever reason, should be utilized in making a revolution. Everyone potentially suited to carry out the task of destruction should be accepted, regardless of his personal motives. To advocate this was the easier for Bakunin because, according to his stern deterministic materialistic view, everyone was only an involuntary product of his environment. This absolved him from any moral obligation. Here, however, it must be said that Bakunin's decision to use criminals in the revolutionary cause was prompted not by his materialistic attitude, but by his desire to see, at any price, the all-destructive revolution and the catastrophe of the existing civilized world. His determinism merely provided a comfortable excuse.

On the hopes Bakunin placed in the criminals, Berdyaev comments:

> The relations between Bakunin and modern Russian Communism are very particular. Disregarding the teachings of Marx, the Communists, as is well known, freed the anarchic, brigand elements of the Russian people in the first period of the Revolution, and made them useful for their own purposes.[82]

[79] Dragomanov, *op. cit.*, p. 235.
[80] Bakunin, *Complete Collection,* II, 256.
[81] Dragomanov, *op. cit.*, p. 498.
[82] Berdiajew, *op. cit.*, pp. 74-75.

This compressed summary is enough to show the extra-ordinary emphasis which Bakunin put on the role of the *déclassé* elements in his scheme of revolution. He considered that their very social position forced them toward revolution and, there-fore, made them into reliable and faithful adherents of the revolution. He expected that in the prerevolutionary stage the *déclassé* educated bourgeois would enlighten the broad masses. He accredited them with the task of transforming the inchoate instincts of opposition of the masses into a conscious desire for an all-embracing revolution.

> Some hundreds of young people with good intentions are, of course, insufficient to organize a revolutionary force apart from the people . . . . But these some hundreds are enough to organize a revolutionary force from among the people.[83]

Bakunin calculated that during the course of the revolution these elements would identify themselves fully with the revolu-tionary cause and would defend it recklessly. He anticipated that the participation of the criminal elements would give to the revolution, in its first stages, that extremely radical, destructive character at which he aimed.

Since Bakunin felt assured of the revolutionary *élan* of the *déclassé* elements, he was anxious about social processes which tended to diminish their number. This was the source of his scathing attacks against the "aristocracy of labor,"[84] and of his repeated pronouncements that, from the point of view of expedi-ency, governmental reprisals of closing the universities were to be welcomed.[85]

As we have already said, all of these revolutionary forces were to be capped, in Bakunin's scheme, by the secret revolu-tionary society. Throughout his life, Bakunin tried to build such secret associations, but in these attempts, he was completely unsuccessful. Continually and tirelessly he elaborated the principles and patterns for such organizations; these found their literary embodiment in his *Revolutionary Catechism, The Cate-chism of the Revolutionary* (called the Nechaev catechism), and in the *Statutes.* Taken together, they are characteristic docu-ments, interesting for more reasons than one and perhaps unique

[83] Quoted in Steklov, *op. cit.,* III, 305.
[84] Maximoff, *op. cit.,* pp. 200-202.
[85] Polonski, *Materialy,* III, 539.

in revolutionary literature. It is true that in them we find much that is meaningless and much that reveals a childish naïveté. But if we disregard this side of the writings, ideas emerge which make us blink our eyes. Since Bakunin's works on these questions are extensive and might provide the basis for a separate study, what is said here will be limited to the essence.

According to Bakunin, a revolutionary conspiracy is unconditionally necessary for the successful leadership of a revolution. This is true not only of the prerevolutionary period. Also, during the revolution itself, the conspiracy should remain secret, or at least preserve its distinct exclusive character, and even after the victory of the revolution, it should not be dissolved. The *Statutes* state:

> . . . it shall be maintained and even strengthened during the period of the revolution, for, being among the people and of the people, it shall replace all government and all official dictatorship.[86]

As the reason for the necessity of such an organization, Bakunin stated:

> Since we want a popular revolution, not only for the people but made exclusively by the people—the folk is our army.
> [We might add that the *déclassé* educated bourgeois elements were to provide the officers.]
> We only need to organize a general staff, which will help it [the people] to organize itself.[87]

It is inevitable that a conspiracy should be necessary for a successful revolution.

> If you create this collective, invisible dictatorship, you will win victory; the well-led revolution will be victorious. If not, then not![88]

The secret revolutionary organization was the keystone of Bakunin's scheme of revolution.

At the same time, Bakunin admitted clearly that in itself it was not a sufficient revolutionary factor.

> But what are three thousand men against the united power of the rich classes and the state, against all the states? Absolutely impotent.[89]

[86] Dragomanov, *op. cit.*, p. 508.
[87] Bakunin, *Gesammelte Werke*, III, 105.　　　[88] *Ibid,* III, 99.
[89] *Ibid.*

Therefore, only the broadest possible participation of the masses in the uprising can make a revolution into a reasonable undertaking. Without such behavior by the masses, the starting of a revolution by the secret society would be suicidal. This was the basis of Bakunin's aggressive criticism of Blanqui's approach. Here, it must be said, Bakunin's scheme of revolution clearly differs from the Malapartian style, for instance. But, on the other hand, Bakunin also preached that even the widest uprising of the masses would achieve nothing if it were not skillfully prepared and directed. And this, he believed, could be done successfully only by the secret revolutionary society.

Since Bakunin attached such importance to the role of the secret society, he considered that it must be built with the utmost care. The organization was not to be very numerous; quality was to replace quantity.[90] Therefore, the members must be "devoted, energetic and talented." They should have a "devil in the flesh." Most important of all, revolutionary action was to be their only occupation. The members "must . . . devote their whole existence to the service of the international revolutionary association."[91] This means that they were to be professional revolutionaries, to use a term now well known, but unknown in Bakunin's time. This notion follows from the whole context of his writings on this question. In the first article of the *Catechism of the Revolutionary*, we read:

> The revolutionist is a doomed man. He has no personal interests, no affairs, sentiments, attachments, property, not even a name of his own. Everything in him is absorbed by one exclusive interest, one thought, one passion —the revolution.[92]

Membership in the secret society is not to be open to all comers, but to be based on coöptation after stern scrutiny. Article 12 of the *Catechism* reads:

> The admission into the organization of a new member, who must have proven himself not by words but by deeds, may be effected only by unanimous agreement.[93]

Upon being recruited, the potential member must accept unconditionally the ideological premises of the organization.[94] Disagreement at any point is enough to prevent membership.

[90] *Ibid.*, III, 105.   [91] *Ibid.*, III, 104, 42.
[92] Dragomanov, *op. cit.*, p. 493.   [93] *Ibid.*, p. 495.
[94] Bakunin, *Gesammelte Werke*, III, 30.

The catechumen must make his revolutionary confession, as Bakunin said, "with heart and passion, will and reason." Once accepted, the member must submit completely to the organization. If required, he must even "renounce his own name."[95]

> The individual disappears, and is replaced by an invisible, unknown, omnipresent legion, which acts everywhere and dies and is regenerated every day . . . . The individuals perish but the legion is immortal.[96]

Bakunin drew a parallel to the Jesuit Order:

> You, who like to reflect so much, have you never thought about the main reason for the power and vitality of the Jesuit Order? Shall I tell you what it is? Yes, it lies in the absolute obliteration of the individuals within the will of the organization, within the action of the Society.[97]

Since this was Bakunin's approach, it is no wonder that although the aim of his conspiracy was to help in the achievement of the fullest liberty and freedom, of the complete extinction of any authority, nevertheless within its own ranks it was to preserve the most severe discipline and subordination. The member "must understand that an association with revolutionary purposes must necessarily be a secret association . . . and must be submitted to strict discipline."[98] Therefore, "any act of disorder shall be considered a crime,"[99] and grave cases may be punished with "expulsion combined with delivery to the vengeance of all the members. . . ." If a former member meets such a fate, then all the remaining members, "regardless of family relationship or previous friendship with the culprit, must not only break all connections with him, but also become his bitter enemies and persecutors."[100]

> [Every member] owes the organization the fullest and most complete truth about every thing and every person which may be of interest to it, and must inform it [the organization] immediately of all events of any importance of which he was a witness or which have come to his attention. Although we [the organization] respect the feeling of delicacy of every individual, we make the following absolute rule in every case: from the *International*

[95] *Ibid.*, III, 95.
[96] *Ibid.*, III, 96.
[97] *Ibid.*, III, 97.
[98] *Ibid.*, III, 35.
[99] *Ibid.*, III, 97.
[100] *Ibid.*, III, 37.

> *Council* [the supreme organ] to which a *brother* [member] belongs, there must be nothing kept secret . . . .
>
> He [the member] will give information even if he has to accuse another international brother.[101]

This procedure, as proposed by Bakunin, openly indicates all-embracing spying by the secret organization, and reciprocal spying upon and denunciations of one member by another within the organization.

In turn, every member is obliged to subordinate his outside social and even private life to the duties imposed by the secret society. He must follow to the letter the instructions given by his superiors, and he may not accept any office or make "any public statement of philosophical, political or economic views, or express his social opinions" without the advice of the revolutionary center. Within the organization, each member:

> . . . has not only the right but also the duty to try to make his views prevail, but as soon as the majority of the *Council of the Directorium* [an organ of the society] has, in the name of the highest authority, decided against him, then he has no right to try to influence public opinion in any way in opposition to this supreme decision.[102]

This regulation may surely be called the first formulation of the concept of "democratic centralism" which was to be applied by the Bolsheviks, the method for achieving strict party discipline by apparently subordinating the minority to the majority, but in reality by submitting all to the undeniably despotic leadership of the few.

Bakunin's whole description of a revolutionary brings to mind that of G. Lucàcs in his *Geschichte und Klassenbewusstsein*. According to Lucàcs, it is neither the radicalness of the ends nor the nature of the means of struggle which is decisive for the making of the revolutionary spirit, but the all-embracing, total character of the movement. A revolutionist may be defined as one who sees each of his acts within the frame of the totality and who accomplishes each with regard to the total central idea. The true revolutionist does not know separate spheres; he denies the delimitation between thinking and acting. This conception of Lucàcs is very close to Bakunin's approach.

[101] *Ibid.*, III, 36.   [102] *Ibid.*, III, 37.

Bakunin's organization was to have two kinds of members, regular members, whom Bakunin called "active brothers," and "titular brothers." The regulations set forth above applied chieflly to the active members. Bakunin made the following characterization of the titular members:

> To the first category, that of international titular brothers, belong all men of great intelligence, high position, great fame, or of scholarly, bureaucratic, political or social influence, or finally very wealthy persons, who do accept the basic principles of our Revolutionary Catechism and are genuinely dedicated to them, who are with us in heart and spirit, hopes and wishes, but who, because of age, health, too numerous occupations or affairs, or other special conditions, or because of the exclusively contemplative nature of their spirit, or because an exaggerated innate caution prevents them from dedicating themselves to the service of our society, cannot take an active part in the conspiracy.[103]

Further we learn that:

> The titular brothers shall remain completely outside the actual conspiracy, and while they know the existence and aims, they shall remain absolutely ignorant of its personnel.[104]

In addition, Bakunin stated that the titular members must always "remain in the minority."[105] Still, in Bakunin's eyes, great advantages would accrue to the association from such members, although special tactics were to be employed in making use of them. Bakunin elaborated his instructions in a letter to one of his friends and collaborators. Since this was a personal communication, and not, like the above, a rule of the *Revolutionary Catechism* destined for the general use of all the members, this letter is noticeably more unscrupulous. Bakunin frankly proposed:

> In order to make use of the influential, the brilliant and the mighty, because of their position or talent, to make use of ambitious and vain people, there is a sure means. One should leave to them the appearance of initiative, the honor of invention, the roles which bring glory and hónor, and be satisfied, not for oneself but for

[103] *Ibid.*, III, 41.   [104] *Ibid.*, III, 42.   [105] *Ibid.*, III, 41.

the entire *Alliance* [the name of the organization], with
the reality of action and power.[106]

While praising such an approach, Bakunin at the same time
warned that only "an inwardly strong group may use such a
method without danger."[107]

If we substitute for Bakunin's term of "titular brother" the
modern one of "fellow traveler," we will at once understand
better what he had in mind for this category of membership.
One is surprised by the accuracy with which Bakunin defined
the essence of this corollary of any modern totalitarian movement and by the clearness and cynicism with which he sketched
the method for making use of this element in the revolutionary
task.

The *Catechism of the Revolutionary*, the so-called Nechaev
Catechism, presents a further sharpening of Bakunin's revolutionary approach and of the tactics to be applied by a revolutionary conspiracy. In this unsurpassable document of revolutionary literature, the nihilistic and negative passions are elevated to the heights of madness:[108]

> The revolutionist despises every sort of doctrinairism
> and has renounced the peaceful scientific pursuits, leaving
> them to future generations. He knows only one science,
> the science of destruction. For this and only this purpose
> he makes a study of mechanics, physics, chemistry, and
> possibly medicine .... The object is but one; the quickest
> possible destruction of that ignoble system. (Art. 5)

> He despises public opinion. He despises and hates
> the present day code of morals with all its motivations
> and manifestations. To him whatever aids the triumph
> of the revolution is ethical; all that which hinders it is
> unethical and criminal. (Art. 4)

> He is not a revolutionist if he is attached to anything
> in this world, if he can stop before the annihilation of
> any situation, relation or person belonging to this world
> —everybody and everything must be equally hateful for
> him. (Art. 13)

---

[106] *Ibid.*, III, 104.   [107] *Ibid.*

[108] The authorship of this *Catechism* was the subject of lively controversy.
Bakunin's faithful followers indignantly repudiated any suggestion that
he might have written the "Nechaev Catechism." However, later
research does not leave any doubt on this point. Cf. B. Kozmin,
P.N. Tkachev i revolyutionnoye dvizheniye 1860-kh godov (Moscow,
1922, pp. 190ff.; Steklov, *op. cit.*, III, 473-479.

The relationship of the revolutionist to his companions should be dictated exclusively by revolutionary expediency.

> The measure of friendship, devotion and other obligations towards such a comrade is determined solely by the degree of his usefulness to the cause of the all-destructive revolution. (Art. 8)

Although the solidarity of the revolutionists is what gives them strength, even that should be given up if revolutionary action requires.

> If a comrade comes to grief, in deciding the question whether or not to save him, the revolutionist must take into consideration not his personal feelings, but solely the interests of the revolutionary cause. (Art. 11)

The same bold, cynical revolutionary expediency is to determine the attitude of the revolutionaries toward society. We learn that the upper class of the contemporary (bourgeois) society (strictly speaking, the *Catechism* takes into account Russian society) should be divided into six categories. The first group is composed of those:

> . . . who are condemned to death without delay. The association should draw up a list of persons thus condemned . . . . (Art. 15)

> In making up such lists . . . one should by no means be guided by the personal villainy of the individual . . . . This villainy and this hatred may even be partly useful by helping to arouse the masses to revolt. It is necessary to be guided by the measure of usefulness which would result, from his death, to the revolutionary cause. (Art. 16)

> [The fourth group] consists of ambitious officeholders and liberals of various shades. One may conspire with them in accordance with their programs, making them believe that one follows them blindly and at the same time one should take hold of them, get possession of all their secrets, compromise them to the utmost, so that no avenue of escape may be left to them, and use them as instruments for stirring up disturbances in the State. Art. 19)

In referring to opponents within the revolutionary camp, the *Catechism* proposed:

> . . . doctrinaires, conspirators, revolutionists talking idly
> in groups or on paper . . . must be continually pushed
> and pulled forward, towards practical, neck-breaking
> statements, the result of which would be the complete
> destruction of the majority and the real revolutionary
> training of the few. (Art. 20)[109]

The *Catechism of the Revolutionist,* together with numerous
pronouncements dispersed in Bakunin's other writings, clearly
establish what may be called revolutionary Machiavellianism,
certainly " Machiavellianism" in the popular meaning of this
word.

As is true of all other problems, Bakunin's views on this
subject are not developed in a systematic manner, but appear
in the form of remarks on particular situations or as the approach
to given tasks. Still, these taken together do form one complex,
and in the case of the *Catechism,* we have a small literary
product completely devoted to this issue.

The essence of Bakunin's revolutionary Machiavellianism is
created by the presumption that whenever there is a conflict
between revolutionary expediency and morals, the latter should
always retreat. Revolutionary expediency must always prevail.
Bakunin's conclusion was not only that the revolutionary conspiracy should not disdain to use immoral means, but that it
would be impossible for it to renounce them. Hence, for Bakunin, revolutionary conspiracy and Machiavellianism were inseparably linked.

This attitude of Bakunin's did not mean that he was blind
to imponderable forces in politics, and especially in the revolutionary cause, but these imponderabilia were still merely forces
for him. Bakunin was not unaware of the importance of morals
and frequently called attention to them, but he was interested
only in a single end, revolution, and indifferent to all others.

All of this gives good reason for considering Bakunin as the
founder, or at least as the most eminent exponent, of revolutionary Machiavellianism. This side of his teaching, no matter
how much it influenced the practice of revolutionary movements directly or indirectly, deserves greater attention than has
generally been given it.

Returning after this digression to Bakunin's schemes for

---

[109] An English translation of the *Catechism of the Revolutionist* is to be
found in Max Nomad, *Apostles of Revolution,* pp. 228-233.

organizing a secret society, we should add that the revolutionary conspiracy was to have an international, global character. It was to create an "invisible net . . . of the devoted revolutionists of all of Europe," and "as far as possible, also of America."[110] For reasons of practical efficiency, the organization was to be divided along national lines. These national sections were to be directed by a single revolutionary center. But, although the ultimate socio-political order which Bakunin postulated was to embody the principle of federation and local autonomy as widely as possible, no trace of this is to be found in the pattern of the secret society. Here, rigid centralization was to reign. The *Statutes* resolved that the component sections "must be organized in such a way that they always remain submitted to the absolute direction of the *International Family* [central board]."[111] The statutes of these national sections might "differ in secondary points," but the "essential and fundamental points must be equally binding and therefore common to all the national sections."[112] And yet, one of the duties of the individual members of the national sections was to be the following:

> [The members of the national section] will spare no efforts and no methods to make the power of the *Society* more secure in their countries and to submit their countries absolutely to the supreme direction of the international power.[113]

So Bakunin envisaged the organizational structure of the revolutionary secret society and the principles and methods of its actions. He assigned the most important revolutionary tasks to it. In the prerevolutionary period, it was to transform the rebellious instincts of the masses into a conscious will to abolish the existing order. It was to create the center of revolutionary propaganda and, by skillfully prepared revolutionary action, to accelerate the outbreak of revolution.

> Above all, what a well organized secret society can do, to help at the birth of a revolution, is to spread among the masses of the people ideas which correspond with their instincts, and to organize, not the army of the revolution —which must be the people—but a sort of revolutionary general staff.[114]

[110] Bakunin, *Gesammelte Werke*, III, 92.   [111] *Ibid.*, III, 29.
[112] *Ibid.*, III, 50.   [113] *Ibid.*, III, 36.   [114] *Ibid.*, III, 90.

Once the revolution breaks out, the secret organization must at once contrive to obtain the uncontestable leadership. Therefore, it must:

> . . . if possible, draw itself even closer together in the first days of the revolution, in order to organize the anarchy [in the sense of confusion] and the fearful unchaining of the revolutionary instincts of the masses, without repressing them. It must imprint upon the revolutionary movement of every land that character of universality without which a movement cannot maintain itself for long, and must finally miscarry.[115]

The secret organization must achieve its ends not by opposing the instincts of the masses in rebellion but by skillfully manipulating them so as to yoke them to the revolution. In the ocean of confusion of the revolution, in the midst of elemental upheavals and convulsions, it must be the sole element which does not lose its political goals from sight. Like an experienced sailor, it must know how to make use of even contrary winds in order to come to harbor.

The task of the secret organization was not to end with the accomplishment of complete pan-destruction, not even with the victorious abolition of the bourgeois social order.

> . . . After the revolution the members will retain and consolidate their organization, so that in their solidarity their combined action may replace an official dictatorship.[116]

This pronouncement by Bakunin was not an empty phrase. It meant that the task of building the new social order and finally of building the new state (we should not be confused by Bakunin's term "anarchy") was to belong, primarily if not exclusively, to the conspiratorial society. The masses of the people, even after the successful abolition of the old order, were to continue to be pliable material in the hands of the new social constructors, recruited exclusively from the revolutionary élite.

In his four volume biography of Bakunin, Steklov, who limited his attention to Bakunin's postulate that for a victorious revolution a disciplined secret organization is necessary, and who did not go into detail about Bakunin's organizational

---

[115] *Ibid.*, III, 82-83.   [116] *Ibid.*, III, 82.

scheme and principles of action, made the following remark on this question:

> The idea that for the preparation and success of a revolution it is necessary to have a disciplined organization, united in theory and practical action—this idea which is at the base of Bakunin's organizational plan, undoubtedly has great positive significance and appears as a serious step forward in comparison with the ideological confusion and organizational chaos prevalent at that time . . . . It appears like a preview of the organizational forms which were first elaborated by the Russian Communists, and afterwards gradually adopted by the other parties belonging to the Communist International.[117]

The Course of Revolution

After this exposition of the preconditions for revolution and of the revolutionary forces which are to carry it out, let us turn to a critical examination of the course which Bakunin believed the revolution would or should take. Perhaps the most adequate introduction to this is to be found in a few passages from Bakunin's *Confession*, referring to certain episodes and Bakunin's plans during the March Revolution. This is the case because the passages reproduce in a picturesque way the genuine aura of the course of Bakunin's revolution.

> In Bohemia I wanted a decisive, radical revolution, in a word, one which, even if it were later defeated, would overthrow everything and turn everything upside down, so that after victory the Austrian government would not find anything in its old place . . . . I wanted to expel the whole nobility, the whole of the hostile clergy, and, after confiscating without exception all landed estates, I wanted to distribute a part of them among the landless peasants in order to incite them to revolution, and to use the rest as a source of extraordinary revolutionary income. I wanted to destroy all castles, to burn all files of documents in all of Bohemia without exception, all administrative, legal and governmental papers, and to proclaim all mortgages paid, as well as all other debts not exceeding a certain sum, e.g. one or two thousand gulden. In a word, the revolution I planned

[111] Steklov, *op. cit.*, III, 118-119.

was terrible, unprecedented, although it was directed more against things than against people. (p. 198)

But my plans did not stop there. I wanted to transform all Bohemia into a revolutionary camp, to create a force there capable not only of defending the revolution within the country, but also of taking the offensive outside of Bohemia . . . . (p. 199)

All clubs, newspapers, and all manifestations of a talkative anarchy were to be abolished, all submitted to one dictatorial power. The young people and all ablebodied men, divided into categories according to their character, ability and inclination, were to be sent throughout the country to provide a provisional revolutionary and military organization. (p. 200)

This revolution was to have been directed by a secret society.

[The secret society] was to be composed of three groups, independent of and unacquainted with each other: one for the townspeople, another for the youth, and a third for the peasants. Each of these societies was to adapt its action to the character of the environment in which it was to agitate. Each was to be submitted to a severe hierarchy and absolute discipline. These three societies were to be directed by a secret central committee composed of three, or at the most, five persons. In the case that the revolution was successful, the secret societies were not to be liquidated; on the contrary, they were to be strengthened and expanded, and take their place in the offices of the revolutionary hierarchy. (pp. 208-209)

Such a revolution, not limited to one nationality, would, by its example and its fiery propaganda, attract not only Moravia, but . . . in general all adjacent German territories . . . . (p. 199)

In regard to Russia, Bakunin had the following plans:

I wanted a republic, but what kind of republic? Not a parliamentary one! . . . I believe that in Russia, more than anywhere else, a strong dictatorial power will be indispensable, but one which would concern itself solely with raising the standard of living and education of the peasant masses; a power free in direction and spirit, but without parliamentary rights; printing books expressing the ideas of freedom, but without freedom of the press; surrounded by the unanimous people, hallowed by their *soviets,* strengthened by their free activity, but unlimited by anything or anybody. (pp. 173, 179)[118]

As we see, these passages reveal the embryonic existence of almost all the essential elements and factors of the social insurrection which Bakunin was to postulate. They show that by the time of the March Revolution, Bakunin's concept of revolution was already mature. During the later years of his life, Bakunin was only to give a generalized application to these premises, to make them more concrete, and to add more details, as well as to provide an ideological justification. They did not, however, undergo any essential revision.

Since we have discussed the moment at which a revolution may break out, let us now proceed to an exposition of the course which Bakunin expected a revolution to take, taking into account all of his other writings.

Let us once again emphasize the fact that, in Bakunin's view, revolution was the only suitable means for achieving social transformation. Existing social reality did not leave open any other possible solution than that of violent revolution. Therefore, any political doctrine or movement which disregarded revolution or considered it merely as an alternative but not the exclusive means for social transformation was considered as wrong by Bakunin and was rejected vigorously.

A complete and radical changing of society, which shall inevitably bring about the abolition of all privileges, monopolies and existing powers, of course cannot be accomplished by peaceful means.[119]

The revolution which Bakunin foresaw was to be "social"; that is, it was to aim at the decisive and total reconstruction of society. First of all, it was to create a completely new economic order, one without exploitation; then a political one, without domination; finally, it was also to accomplish a moral regeneration of society by changing its spiritual *Weltanschauung.* Therefore, a merely political revolution, which only tries to create a new and different political system, is never sufficient and indeed is worthless.

Any exclusively political revolution, whether a national one directed exclusively against foreign domination, or an

---

[118] Bakunin's *Confession,* as printed in Polonski's *Materialy,* I, 198, 199, 200, 208, 209, 173, 179.
[119] Bakunin, *Gesammelte Werke,* III, 33.

internal one aiming at constitutional reform, even if its goal is a republic, will be, since its chief aim is not the immediate and real political and economic liberation of the people, a betraying, lying, impossible, pernicious, regressive and counter-revolutionary revolution.[120]

Therefore only a "social revolution" is a reasonable undertaking, one worthy of the effort expended. It must be at the same time a "philosophical, political, economic and social revolution."[121] The revolution must have two sides. As defined in *Revolutionary Principles,* the first stage should embrace "the period of the destruction of existing forms by rendering them amorphous"; the second, "the creation of completely new forms out of this amorphism." The lack of a clear, detailed program for the future order is not an obstacle to the making of a "social revolution." Indeed, such an objection can only be raised by "dilettantes or Philistines."[122]

The negative side of the revolution was to be limited to the complete abolition of the existing reality; its positive side was to cover the complete emancipation of the worknig masses and the creation of a new social order, securing liberty and equality. The period of revolution, therefore, was to embrace not only the stage of destruction but also the period of the recasting of society. The revolution lasts until this reconstruction has been completed and the re-education of society on the new ideological basis accomplished. In this way, revolution becomes a very long, almost unending process, without a clear point of termination. As the revolution runs its course, a new factor is added, that of the re-education and spiritual remodeling of society. Gradually, this factor becomes more important, and it ends by becoming predominant over all the others.

Finally, Bakunin's revolution was to be "universal," "cosmopolitan." It should not be limited to any one country or nation, but must be a world revolution or at least an all-European one. This was necessary for the simple reason that the alliance of "reactionary forces" was well organized and unified. In a phrase, there was a "world reaction."[123]

> Against this world reaction the isolated revolution of a single people cannot succeed. It would be a folly, and

---

[120] *Ibid.,* III, 52. [121] *Ibid.,* III, 81.
[122] Dragomanov, *op. cit.,* p. 479.
[123] Bakunin, *Gesammelte Werke,* III, 28.

consequently a mistake, on the part of this people, and a betrayal of, a crime against all other peoples. From now on the insurrection of a people must be carried out not with regard to that people alone, but to the whole world.[124]

Of course, one cannot expect that the revolution will start simultaneously, at an exactly synchronized moment, in all countries. A revolution would start in a specific territory or place. But it should have a good chance of spreading all over, and from its onset, it should endeavor to achieve a universal character.

In order that a revolution take on such a character, it is first of all necessary, in Bakunin's opinion, that it have a suitably universal program.

So that a nation may arise in the name of the whole world, it must have a program for the whole world—a sufficiently broad, deep, true, in a word a sufficiently human, program, one which includes the interests of all and will electrify the passions of all the masses of Europe, without regard to nationality. . . . Such a program is to be found only in the democratic and social revolution.[125]

Another way to give the required universal character to the revolution is to provide the leadership of the international secret association.

In this way, by the [common] idea and the same common program for all lands, [the revolution must be] centralized, and also centralized by a secret organization, which will unite in a single plan of action, not only all the parts of a land, but also many if not all lands, even through the simultaneity of the revolutionary movement in many places in the country and the city . . . .[126]

In this way, revolution would have the "necessary local character" and also be a feature of a well organized, centralized action. It should never turn into a "Romanesque expedition" by the members of the secret revolutionary organization (an allusion to Garibaldi's tactics), since this would be a complete failure. It must have the character of a general uprising of the broad masses of the people since "only a revolution among the

---

[124] *Ibid.*, III, 29.   [125] *Ibid.*   [126] *Ibid.*, III, 52.

masses is true, just, and real."[127] Even "women, old people, and children should take part in it."[128]

> It remains well understood that the first land that is fortunate enough to make a victorious revolution will at once become a center of propaganda and revolutionary activity for all lands, and that it will hasten to offer its entire support and all the material means necessary for success.[129]

In summary of Bakunin's reasoning about the necessity of a social and international character for the future revolution, let us cite the following quotation:

> No revolution can count on success if it does not speedily spread beyond the individual nation to all other nations. A political and national revolution cannot, therefore, be victorious unless the political revolution becomes social, and the national revolution, because of its fundamentally socialistic and state-destroying character, becomes universal.[130]

It must always be kept in mind that the revolution which Bakunin postulated was to have two stages. In the first, that devoted to the complete abolition of the existing order, the revolution was to be a violent rebellion of the outraged masses, including the women, the aged, and the children. It was to be an unparalleled mutiny, born of indignation against oppression and exploitation. Technically, a social revolution must be a simultaneous revolt of the city workers and the peasants. Both must take part in the uprising from the very beginning; "an uprising by the proletariat alone would not be enough."[131] Therefore, the revolutionaries "should use all the means at their disposal to break the ice separating the proletariat of the cities from the people of the villages, and to unite and organize these two classes into one."[132]

From the first day, the revolution must make itself manifest by the destruction of everything which it is at all possible to destroy of the existing order. "It shall not leave one stone upon another, over the entire earth."[133] The slogan should be: "Peace to the workers, freedom to the oppressed, death to the

---

[127] *Ibid.*, III, 233. [128] *Ibid.*, III, 52. [129] *Ibid.*, III, 83.
[130] *Ibid.*, III, 91. [131] Bakunin, *Works, Golos Truda* ed., IV, 202.
[132] Maximoff, *op. cit.*, p. 205.
[133] Bakunin, *Gesammelte Werke,* III, 85.

masters and exploiters."[134] It was Bakunin's opinion that the more destruction there was, the better; if only for the reason that by this destruction of the old system, any return to it would be impossible or at least extremely difficult. For this purpose, an appeal should be made to the baser instincts of the masses, and the criminals should be called in to help. These base instincts should be given a free outlet. This was the basis for Bakunin's admission that "by revolution we understand the unchaining of everything that today is called 'evil passions,' and the destruction of everything that is called in the same language, 'public order.'"[135] Although Bakunin acknowledges that this negative passion certainly does not rise to the level of the revolutionary cause, still he considers that:

> . . . without that passion the revolutionary cause is impossible of realization, for there can be no revolution without a sweeping and passionate destruction, a salutary and fruitful destruction, since by means of such a destruction new worlds are born and come into existence.[136]

If the objection had been raised that such a situation would also have brought a paralysis of society, Bakunin would probably not have denied it. Indeed, from the point of view of revolutionary expediency, he would have considered this as useful. He declared: "We are not afraid of anarchy [here—confusion], we call upon it."[137] An answer to the question of who Bakunin's "we" is clarifies the whole matter. The "we" is the secret revolutionary society which, it will be remembered, was to draw itself even more tightly together in the first days of the revolution.[138] As long as there was on the one hand a well-organized, closely-knit secret association and on the other the raging confusion, general panic, and total destruction brought about by the base instincts of the masses, the revolution would be safe. As long as the confusion did not touch the secret society (and it was supposed to be impervious), there was, in Bakunin's eyes, no reason for embarrassment. On the contrary, the secret society, an island in the ocean of disorder and panic, would find its task the easier because this situation would paralyze its foes, the adherents of the old order, and its new, potential antagonists. It would leave the incontestable domination of the revolutionary situation to the conspiracy. This is

---

[134] *Ibid.*   [135] *Ibid.*, III, 88.   [136] Maximoff, *op. cit.*, p. 381.
[137] Bakunin, *Gesammelte Werke*, III, 88.   [138] *Ibid.*, III, 82.

why Bakunin stated: "The aim of our association is to drive the masses into making a *tabula rasa* . . . ."[139] "We must bring forth anarchy, and be its invisible pilots . . . ."[140]

In speaking of Bakunin's recipe, Masaryk made a comparison:

> In fact, Bakunin and his Social Democracy comes to the same result to which the outspoken aristocrat Renan came with his ingenious machine. This machine could wreck the world except the intellectual elite which, alone in knowing its secret mechanism, kept the masses in fear and subordination. Bakunin invents not an all-destroying machine, but an all-destructive revolution, which is to be kept under the direction of the elite of his secret society.[141]

This revolutionary politics of demoniac destruction was to have one primary trend, the immediate abolition and liquidation of the state. Inexorably, Bakunin repeats this revolutionary commandment over and over and stresses with all his inborn passion that "in the destruction of the state lies the whole secret of revolution."[142] He proposed a whole series of steps to be taken to destroy the state effectively: cessation of state collection of private debts, payment of which was to be left to the debtors' pleasure; cessation of the payment of taxes and all levies, direct or indirect; dissolution of the army, the courts, the civil service, the police, and the clergy; termination of official administration of justice; abolition of everything that is called juridical rights and their exercise; hence the voiding and consignment to an *auto-da-fé* of all titles to property, testamentary dispositions, bills of sale, deeds of gift, and judgments of courts. At every turn "revolutionary fact" was to step into the place of the law created and guaranteed by the state. All capital goods and instruments of production were to be confiscated for the use of labor associations, which were to use them for collective production. All church and state property, and all bullion in private hands were to be promptly confiscated.[143] All archives and documents were to be burned.[144]

> The revolution will begin with the destruction of all the edifices and offices which go to make up the existence

139 *Ibid.*, III, 109.
140 Quoted in M. Nettlau, *Der Anarchismus* (Berlin, 1927), p. 150.
141 Masaryk, *op. cit.*, II, 23.
142 Bakunin, *Gesammelte Werke*, III, 87.
143 *Ibid.*, III, 88.   144 *Ibid.*, III, 53.

of the state: churches, parliaments, courts, administrations, armies, banks, universities, etc. The state must be destroyed completely and declared bankrupt, not only financially, but also politically, bureaucratically, militarily, judicially and in regard to the police.[145]

Thus, Bakunin's idea was that the bourgeois state must be demolished completely, a *Staatszerstörungstheorie,* as Cunow calls it.[146] The new social order can be built, according to this view, only after the complete abolition of the previous one. An effort to create a new social order will be doomed to failure if it attempts to transform old social institutions to meet new demands. These old institutions must be destroyed completely before the new construction is begun. Social progress cannot be secured by any mere socio-political amelioration, no matter how extensive, if the old institutions, however much transformed, are left. They must be obliterated. The precondition for the new, ideal world is the razing to the ground of the old one.

Since the state is the embodiment of the old reality, it must be eradicated first of all. Therefore, revolutionary forces must not aim at obtaining power, even in a revolutionary way, within the institution of the previous state. On the contrary, they must completely destroy these old state institutions and start building the new social reality completely afresh.

The idea that the destruction of the bourgeois state was the most important precondition for the erecting of the new order was later to be developed at length by Lenin in his pamphlet, *The State and Revolution.* Lenin affirmed that this view was shared by Marx and stated: "This conclusion is the chief and fundamental point in the Marxian teaching on the state." He also said that "the similarity of views on this point between Marxism and anarchism (both Proudhon and Bakunin) neither the opportunists nor the Kautskyites wish to see . . . ."[147]

Without going into the lively controversy between the western Socialists and the Bolsheviks about this question, we may remember that Cunow called the Bolshevik view "a relapse into Bakuninism."[148] Vyshinsky, in his *The Law of the Soviet State,* repeated after Lenin that "the most important problem of the Marxist-Leninist doctrine of the state is that of demolish-

---

[145] *Ibid.*   [146] Cunow, *op. cit.,* I, 331.
[147] V. I. Lenin, *The State and Revolution* (Moscow, 1951), pp. 47, 86.
[148] Cunow, *op. cit.,* I, 335.

ing the machinery of the bourgeois state." Then he proceeded to an attack on the divergent views of the western Socialist theoreticians:

> Is it an accident that the most vulgar and ignoble renegades of Marxism—like the Kautskys, the Cunows, and the Adlers—fall in such fury and frenzy upon this doctrine of Marx relative to the demolition of the state machine?[149]

The question of the extent to which a demand for the demolition of the existing state may be ascribed to the teaching of Marx is one which does not belong to our theme. But it is unquestionable that, in Bakunin's pattern of revolution, this is the cornerstone. This idea had already come to full growth in Bakunin's mind during the March Revolution. After that, he never left it, and indeed he spent the rest of his life in propagating it with all his passion and uncompromising energy.

In summary of Bakunin's notion of the course of revolution, let us recapitulate: the revolution was to be manifested in elemental unrestrained upheavals of the masses of the people, skillfully and invisibly directed by the secret revolutionary association. These explosive popular outbursts were to be turned to demolition, creating total social confusion, disorder, and panic. The main object to be demolished was the state and its institutions, and the culmination of the process was to be the complete eradication of the existing state and old social order.

Bakunin remained firm in this revolutionary goal, but the tactics which he advised were always susceptible to modification. He always stressed the need for flexibility here.

We have already seen some of the means which Bakunin advocated: tactics toward the peasantry, or the approach of the revolutionaries toward influential bourgeois or toward dissidents within the revolutionary camp. A curious point is the importance which Bakunin ascribed to conflagrations during the course of the revolution. Indeed, one may be startled by the frequency with which he repeats that all files and documents must be burnt. The Russian revolutionist Debogori-Mokriyevich, who once visited Bakunin in Switzerland, relates in his *Memoirs*

[149] A. Y. Vyshinsky, *The Law of the Soviet State* (New York, 1948), pp. 62, 66, 60.

that Bakunin expressed the conviction that the main cause of the setback to the Barcelona uprising [which took place in 1873] was the failure to burn all administrative and juridical documents and files.[150] An explanation of this wild tendency on Bakunin's part is probably to be found in the rural mentality of the Russian peasants who, in their naïveté, were fetishists toward any sort of written documents. But, regardless of the source of this strange appeal by Bakunin, let us cite Max Weber's opinion as to its efficacy:

> The naïve idea of Bakuninism of destroying the basis of "acquired right" and "domination" by destroying public documents overlooks the settled orientation of *man* for keeping to habitual rules and regulations that continue to exist independently of documents.[151]

Specific attention should be given to two other means to which Bakunin allocated a role in his revolution: propaganda and terrorism.

The whole context of Bakunin's reasoning confirms the impression that he assigned an extremely important role to revolutionary propaganda. For instance, he always urged that, even before the revolution, the secret society should be a center of revolutionary propaganda. But this propaganda was not to be limited to the spoken or printed word, it should be put into practice in deeds; as he said, it should be "activist propaganda."[152]

In the prerevolutionary stage, Bakunin gave to propaganda the task of awakening the masses and transforming their instinctive revolt into a conscious will to abolish the existing order. But propaganda was not to be diminished during the revolution. As we have seen, the first land to achieve a successful revolution was to become a propaganda center.[153] Moreover, he advocated the "sending, not of official commissioners of the revolution wearing some sort of badges, but of revolutionary agitators to all the provinces and communities, and especially to the peasants." And he repeated that the agitators must employ not only words but also "revolutionary deeds."[154]

The agitators were to be skillful, bold, and unscrupulous in their choice of means. Let us see a few of Bakunin's examples.

[150] V. K. Debogori—Mokriyevich, *Vospominaniya*, pp. 94ff.
[151] Max Weber, *op. cit.*, p. 229.
[152] Bakunin, *Gesammelte Werke*, III, 91.
[153] *Ibid.*, III, 83.   [154] *Ibid.*, III, 89.

activity of the revolutionary communes, or to re-establish any of the institutions which are abolished.[163]

This article alone, because of its all-inclusive definitions, may be considered as the *magna carta terroris* of Bakunin's revolution. In addition, we may remember the *Catechism of the Revolutionist* (the Nechaev), which was a sort of guidebook to revolutionary terrorism.

What then was Bakunin's true attitude toward political terror during the revolution? Was his vacillation sincere or dictated by tactical reasons? There is not sufficient evidence to enable us to answer these questions definitely. At this point, Bakunin was continually inconsistent. If the problem was posed in the abstract, he rather rejected and condemned terrorism, but if a concrete situation was involved, then he clearly inclined toward using it.

What is decisive for our discussion, however, is not how Bakunin would have acted personally if he had (let us make the assumption) headed a revolution or what his wishful thinking was, but what conclusions are to be drawn from his ideological premises. Here there is little room for doubt. On the basis of the principles of revolutionary action which he postulated, it was impossible to condemn political terrorism either during the course of the revolution or in the preparatory period. Bakunin condemned political terrorism as an end in itself, but was willing to tolerate it if it were demanded by his never clearly defined "revolutionary expediency," as he said, "to save the men without danger to the revolution."[164]

After the revolution comes the question of the revolutionary morrow. From the fires of rebellion was to arise the phoenix of the new organization of society. Bakunin assures us:

> This new life—the people's revolution—will not delay in organizing itself, but it will pattern its revolutionary organization from below upwards and from the periphery to the center according to the principle of freedom.[165]

We may summarize the main features of the organization which Bakunin prophesied. The basic revolutionary territorial unit, the commune, was to set up a "revolutionary council"

[163] Dragomanov, *op. cit.*, p. 302.
[164] Bakunin, *Gesammelte Werke*, III, 85.   [165] *Ibid.*, III, 88.

composed of delegates elected by the population. This revolutionary council was to form an executive committee with various branches for the "revolutionary administration of the commune." The capital, after successful abolition of the previous authority, was to "renounce the right to govern the provinces and to set a standard for them." The communes were to send delegates to a provincial center to create a provincial revolutionary council and executive committee. Similarly, a federation of provinces should be created in a national group, and in turn there should be a federation of revolutionary nations. In following this procedure, there was no need, Bakunin felt, to adhere to previous political and administrative boundaries. The previous frontiers of the states, provinces, and communes might all be disregarded.[166]

Bakunin's plans for the long period of revolution also provided for revolutionary tribunals. All offices and mandates were to be elective and revocable at any moment. Instructions given by the population to their representatives were to be binding. It clearly appears that the voting system was to be indirect, and that the problem of division between executive and legislative power was disregarded. On the basis of Bakunin's suggestions, it seems clear that certain groups of the population (e.g. the previous bourgeoisie, if it survived the revolution) were to be deprived of the right to vote.[167]

Bakunin constantly emphasized that the new political and administrative system was not to be imposed from above upon the population by a political center but that it should grow up spontaneously from below and voluntarily find federative organizational forms on a higher level. The new governmental machine was to be built in a pyramidal or peripheral manner and should be erected from the bottom up, i.e. beginning with the local communes. However, this did not mean that the constituent administrative entities were to become isolated, since this would endanger the revolution. As Bakunin stressed: "No commune can defend itself if it is isolated . . . ."[168] Consequently, he assumed that the need to defend the revolution would impel the revolutionary communes, provinces, and nations toward a tight union. And, as we have seen, the first successfully revolutionary country was to become the center of revolutionary

[166] *Ibid.*, III, 53, 88, 89.
[167] *Ibid.*, III, 53, 88, 12, 51.   [168] *Ibid.*, III, 53.

propaganda and activity for all the other lands and offer them support in their struggle.[169]

A volunteer army was to be created to defend the revolution.[170]

These revolutionary political and administrative institutions and structures were what might be called the proposed official, outward forms of organization of the masses of the people. But we must not forget that other revolutionary factor, the secret society. According to Bakunin, this important revolutionary force was to continue to be exclusive even during and after a successful revolution. It was not to dissolve itself within the official revolutionary apparatus but was to preserve and even strengthen its separate organization, becoming the sole real driving and guiding force behind the curtain of the visible, official governmental institutions and offices. As Bakunin said:

> During and after the revolution (as before) the members will preserve and consolidate their organization, in order to replace with their common and combined activity any official dictatorship.[171]

This was the pattern of the revolution and its aftermath which Bakunin suggested and expected. It is hardly necessary to point out the degree to which Bakunin's plans coincide with Bolshevik practice. The similarity is so striking that a detailed analysis would be superfluous.

Steklov, himself a prominent participant in the Bolshevik Revolution, after examining Bakunin's revolutionary pattern only on the basis of the *Confession* (though his conclusions were to be reinforced by further study), remarks with genuine rapture:

> But the most striking aspect of Bakunin's plan lies in the fact that at many points it anticipates the existence of Soviet power, and foresees in general lines the course of the Great Russian October Revolution of 1917. In this sense it seems like a colossal historic prophecy, and this fact alone gives Bakunin the right to be immortalized in the memory of the Russian and the international proletariat . . . . In his project, Bakunin develops the scheme of a popular revolution. Which one? Anarchist—will

169 *Ibid.*, III, 83.
170 *Ibid.*, III, 84.
171 *Ibid.*

exclaim his devoted followers. No—we repeat, not anarchist but rather communist . . . . This is not anarchism
in the particular meaning of this word, but rather Soviet
power, dictatorship of the proletariat.[172]

And, we may remark, in this instance Steklov was completely
correct.

Leaving the discussion of the problem of statism within the
future anarchist order to the next chapter, let us only say here
that, in terms of power, the political organization of society
which Bakunin postulated during and after the revolution was
still, of course, a state. And even Bakunin, despite his vitriolic
anti-state terminology and his continuous assurances to the
contrary, in a moment of frankness once called it "a new and
revolutionary state."[173] But his fundamental motto remained:
"If there is a state, then there is domination, and in turn there
is slavery."[174]

Therefore, one may say that Bakunin's attitude toward
revolution is colored by that orgiastic chiliasm which "sees the
revolution as a value in itself, not as an unavoidable means to a
rationally set end, but as the only creative principle of the
immediate present, as the longed-for realization of its aspirations
in this world."[175]

[172] Steklov, *op. cit.,* I, 343-345.
[173] Bakunin, *Gesammelte Werke,* III, 90.
[174] Bakunin, *Works, Golos Truda* ed., I, 233.
[175] Karl Mannheim, *Ideologie und Utopie* (2nd ed., Bonn, 1930), p. 199.

CHAPTER 6

THE FUTURE ANARCHIST ORDER
Liberty and Equality

IT IS only too often true of social reformers that, however great their critical and destructive abilities, they seem unable to develop a clear constructive program. Their picture of the desired future order is drawn less in terms of what it will be than of what it will not be. However, this method does not allow an exact opposite to be deduced from the negative, and the obscurity remains extensive.

This certainly applies to Bakunin. In describing the future anarchist order, he had much less to say than he had had in condemning the existing one, and incomparably less than he had to say about the destruction of the latter by revolution. Apparently little disturbed by this, he attempted to present his position as a normal one.

> We frankly refuse to work out plans for future conditions, because this does not coincide with our activity, and therefore we consider the purely theoretical work of reasoning as useless.[1]

It is also true that he said that "no one can aim at destruction without having at least a remote conception, whether true or false, of the new order," but we learn immediately that the reason for having such a conception is that this aids in fomenting destruction, since, "the more vividly the future is visualized, the more powerful is the force of destruction."[2] Thus, Bakunin falls back into the well-worn grooves of his thought. Therefore, even this apparent deviation does not really differ in sense from Bakunin's repeated pronouncement: "For those who are already committed to the cause of revolution, all talk about the distant

[1] Quoted in Steklov, *op. cit.*, III, 454, 455.
[2] Bakunin, *Works, Golos Truda* ed., V, 36.

future is criminal because it hinders pure destruction and stems the tide of revolution."[3]

On the whole, then, Bakunin, like the later syndicalists, gave but little thought to the elaboration of the details of the future society, a neglect quite in accordance with his contempt for idle prophecies, for the spinning of dreams, and for all that savors of utopia. Bakunin was proud of advocating and organizing a movement depending on action rather than on speculation, on "prophetic mania." But at the same time it appears that he was not always able to resist his prophetic impulses. We find scattered pronouncements in his writings which give a basis for general agreement as to the chief aspects of the future anarchist order which he proposed.

As the point of departure for the future anarchist order, Bakunin took two ideals, freedom and equality, which he brought into an inseparable reciprocal interdependence. They were to provide a compass for the creation of a new, anarchist, ideal society. They were also the causes of the fact that the total destruction of the existing order was considered not only as an excusable undertaking, but also as an obligatory moral commandment.

Here Bakunin's doctrine of anarchism met a perennial problem of political philosophy. At one pole of political thought stands the presumption that freedom and equality contradict each other, that equality can only come from the coercion of authority, and that freedom, on the other hand, includes the freedom to be unequal. At the other pole is the equalitarian doctrine that liberty and equality are complementary and inseparable, that liberty implies equality, that the realization of the first presupposes the realization of the second, and that both are but two different facets of the same ideals. Between these two poles there is a wide range for compromise solutions, both in theory and in practice.

Bakunin discussed this problem readily and frequently However, many of his repeated pronouncements are mere rhetoric which we need not consider here.

In looking first at Bakunin's idea of freedom, we must stress that, in his view, liberty must operate within the framework of necessity, or, as Bakunin puts it, of "nature" and "society." The exercise of freedom depends upon the recognition of this fact.

[3] Dragomanov, *op. cit.*, p. 480.

Man can never be altogether free in relation to natural
and social laws. What is freedom? What is slavery?
Does man's freedom consist in revolting against all laws?
We say no, in so far as laws are natural, economic and
social laws, [laws] not authoritatively imposed but inherent in things, in relations, in situations, the natural
development of which is expressed by those laws.[4]

However, Bakunin's logic does not give us any workable
criteria for distinguishing between "natural" and "artificial," or,
as he calls them, "political and juridical" laws. Therefore, these
premises are not enough to take us far in defining his notion of
liberty. Bakunin does offer a few direct definitions of liberty.

Freedom is the absolute right of all adult men and
women to seek permission for their actions only from
their own conscience and reason, and to be determined
in their actions only by their own will, and consequently
to be responsible only to themselves, and then to the
society to which they belong, but only insofar as they
have made a free decision to belong to it.[5]

What is the true basis of and the positive condition
for freedom? It is each person's fullest development and
enjoyment of all his physical, spiritual, and moral capaci-
ties. Consequently, provision must be made for all the
material means which are necessary to human existence,
and also for education and instruction.

The negative condition of freedom is the following.
No man owes obedience to another. Man is only free
under the condition that all his actions are determined,
not by the will of another, but by his own will and his
own convictions.[6]

Such a definition of freedom is certainly not unambiguous.
It does, however, at least approximate the following interpretation: freedom means the utmost absence of restraints. But
this is not all. It also requires a positive and equal opportunity
for, to use a rather vague phrase, the self-realization of the
individual.

From this, it may appear that Bakunin's conception of liberty
resembles that of individualism. This is certainly not the case.
Bakunin used strong words to condemn individualism as a

[4] Maximoff, *op. cit.*, p. 263.
[5] Bakunin, *Gesammelte Werke*, III, 9.
[6] *Ibid.*, II, 244-245.

doctrine of unrestrainted egoism, the application of which leads to the war of each against all.[7] Since Bakunin rejected the entire substratum of an individualistic formula of liberty, it is impossible to interpret his conception of liberty in this manner. Moreover, he directly protested the interpretation of his concept of liberty as individualism in the sense of the unrestrained ego (to use a later term) getting its own way, as was the notion in Stirner's anarchism and solipsism. To guard against that, Bakunin stated:

> The freedom of every man is the real result, produced ever anew, by a multitude of physical, mental, and moral influences to which he is subjected by the environment in which he lives and dies. To wish to escape from this influence, in the name of a transcendental, divine freedom, self-sufficient and absolutely egoistic, is to aim at nonexistence. This notorious independence, so greatly extolled by the idealists and metaphysicians, and individual freedom conceived in this sense, are just mere nothingness.[8]

Elsewhere Bakunin stated:

> Society . . . indeed first creates freedom for human individuals. Society is the root, the tree, freedom its fruit.[9]
>
> The individuality of the human being is the product of solidarity, i.e. of society.[10]
>
> It is so much the worse for those who are sufficiently ignorant of the natural and social laws of human solidarity as to imagine that the absolute mutual independence of individuals or of the masses is possible or desirable.[11]

In a fragmentary variant of Bakunin's *Statutes* of his secret society (found among the papers of Peter Kropotkin and first published in 1926), we see that this stress on solidarity goes extremely far.

> Social solidarity is to be the first human law; liberty is the second law of society. These two laws complement each other and are inseparable from each other, and together they constitute the entire essence of humanity.

[7] *Ibid.*, II, 257ff.
[8] Maximoff, *op. cit.*, p. 264.
[9] Bakunin, *Complete Collection*, I, 9.
[10] Bakunin, *Works, Golos Truda* ed., IV, 57.
[11] *Ibid.*, V, 48.

Thus freedom is not the negation of solidarity. On the contrary, it represents the development of, and, if it is possible to say so, the humanization of the latter.[12]

Through Bakunin's extraordinary emphasis on solidarity, his concept of freedom shows an obvious moral tint. Indeed, this permits him to consider sociology as a branch of ethics. Social life is to be arranged primarily in accordance with moral principles, which are the emanation of reason and conscience.

At this point, we might well remember that Bakunin's formula of liberty allows one to draw political conclusions like those of Aksakov. As we have mentioned, Aksakov was one of the leading representatives of the Russian Slavophile school and an advocate of a semi-anarchist doctrine which may perhaps best be defined as conservative anarchism. The aim of this was a moral identification between the governing and the governed and not necessarily a stateless society in the strict meaning of this term. Yet, as we shall see, Bakunin's scheme for the future anarchist order, while departing from an individualistic platform, clearly indicates similar socio-political ends. Bakunin's entire ideological sermon is saturated with a more or less tacit assumption of the spontaneous philosophic self-identification of every individual with the whole of society. He repeatedly states that socialism will take the place of a new human religion and that it consequently also provides a new standard of ethics. Within the frame of this new order, the spontaneous identification of each participant with the new ethics will be equivalent to the realization of freedom. In this way, the whole problem of freedom becomes psychological and subjective. Man is free if he feels himself to be free, no matter how objectively restricted or how subject to sacrifice he may be.

However, the most appropriate way of discussing Bakunin's concept of liberty is to interpret it in close connection with his second ideal—equality. He linked them inseparably. According to Bakunin, freedom, in any sense of the term, had no meaning except within the context of equality. He affirmed that "the freedom of each may only be achieved through the equality of all," and that "the realization of freedom, through juridical and real equality," will produce "justice."[13]

---

[12] *Mikhail Bakunin, 1876-1926, Neizdannye materialy i stati* (Moscow, 1926), p. 96.
[13] Bakunin, *Gesammelte Werke,* III, 9.

He asserts that there is a universal impulse toward equality among the masses. As his rhetoric runs on, he states:

> The instinctive passion of the masses for economic equality is so great that if they could hope to receive it from the hands of despotism, they would indubitably and without much reflection do as they have often done before . . . .

Dismayed by such a discovery, Bakunin immediately restricted its meaning by adding:

> "Happily, historic experience has been of some service even with the masses. Today, they are beginning everywhere to understand that no despotism has nor can have either the will or the power to give them economic equality.[14]

On equality, Bakunin had the following to say:

> Equality does not mean the elimination of individual differences, or of the intellectual, moral, and physical identity of individuals. These differences of abilities and talents, of races, nations, and sex . . . make up the wealth of humanity.[15]

What Bakunin aimed at was "to give society an order in which every single man or woman coming into the world may find an equal chance to make use of his ability."[16] One of the consequences of this was Bakunin's demand that the laws of inheritance be abolished.

One side of this reasoning approaches the ideas of the Saint-Simonian school; the other echoes bourgeois tradition with its demand for equality of opportunity. This latter would, however, be a false interpretation of Bakunin's second ideal, equality. If a prototype for Bakunin's formula of equality is to be sought, it may be found in Babeuf's ideas. We have mentioned that Bakunin's thought runs parallel to that of Babeuf at many points. This is no accident, for he was enraptured by Buonarotti's book on Babeuf's conspiracy, recommending it to his followers. At the Basel Congress of the First International, Bakunin said, "We are his [Babeuf's] successors . . . ." and called Buonarotti "the greatest conspirator of this [the 19th] century."[17]

---

[14] Bakunin, *Marxism, Freedom, and the State,* K. J. Kenafick, ed. (London), p. 61.
[15] Bakunin, *Gesammelte Werke,* III, 19.
[16] Bakunin, *Selected Works,* p. 137.
[17] Steklov, *op. cit.,* III, 370.

In returning to Bakunin's concept of equality, we find that as this emerges from the whole context of his writings, it is in fact a "real equality" in spite of what he says about differentiations. We find an assertion and a demand that, on the whole, each individual is not, and cannot be, different; one is not worth more than another and shall not have more means at his disposal than any other individual. This is a negative definition of his equalitarianism and perhaps the best one.

In Bakunin's writings, we do, however, find certain clues toward a positive formula of equality. First of all, this equality shall be economic. The economic status of all individuals shall be equal. We say economic status rather than wealth, since in Bakunin's anarchist order, wealth is to be collective. Does this mean an equal income for all? Perhaps, but no clearly affirmative answer is possible, since Bakunin made no written statements about income in the future society. Economic equality is the fundamental prerequisite for any equality in Bakunin's scheme. From this premise comes the conclusion that collective property should be established and the law of inheritance abolished.

We may ask whether, in Bakunin's view, economic equality was the only precondition for the equalitarian anarchist society. He draws a clear distinction between economic and social equality[18] and does not regard the economic power or property of an individual as the only source of inequality. He finds another root in education, which enables a person to achieve a higher position in the social pyramid in spite of his lack of means of production. Therefore, a second requirement for equality is a broad, equal education for all (*l'instruction intégrale*).

> We have demonstrated that as long as there are two or more grades of education for different classes of society, different classes will inevitably exist.
>
> As members of the International, we want equality, and because we want it, we must also want complete equal education for all of you [workers].[19]

Thus, Bakunin's device is: "Everybody must work and everybody must be educated."[20]

[18] Bakunin, *Gesammelte Werke,* II, 106.
[19] *Ibid.,* II, 110.
[20] *Ibid.,* II, 110-111.

The next question which arises is that of political disparity, of inequalities in the political power of the individual. Here, Bakunin's task was a relatively easy one. Since the anarchist order presupposed the abolition of the state and of political power, the abolition of politics totally and forever, this crucial problem simply does not exist in the theoretical schemes of a future anarchist society.

This also answers another question. Did Bakunin anticipate that economic equality, even combined with equal education, might still fail to guarantee political freedom in a non-anarchist society? The answer is affirmative. It can be seen in the above statement to the effect that the masses would be ready to accept equality even from the hands of despots. And elsewhere we are told that "freedom without socialism is privilege and injustice, and socialism without freedom is slavery and brutality."[21]

On the subject of the natural inequalities among individuals, Bakunin believed that these were rooted in economic and social inequalities and that they would steadily diminish in an equalitarian, anarchist society.

> Inequalities among individuals, which arise from differences of talent, ability, and productive energy, will, without ever disappearing completely, steadily diminish under the influence of an education and social organization founded on equality.[22]

Bakunin's notion of equality was, on the whole, in accordance with the general trend of socialist thought of his time. He used a moral argument in favor of the necessity of equality, namely that it would allow the free development of the individual in society. But he also used a natural proof:

> From the naturalistic point of view, all men are equal. There are only two exceptions to this rule of naturalistic equality: geniuses and idiots. But these exceptions do not invalidate the rule, and in general one may say that all human individuals are equal.[23]

We now arrive at the question of the correlation of these two ideals, liberty and equality, in Bakunin's doctrine of anarchism. We have said that they were brought into reciprocal

[21] Bakunin, *Works, Golos Truda* ed., III, 147.
[22] Bakunin, *Gesammelte Werke,* III, 20.
[23] *Ibid.,* II, 249.

interdependence, and though not considered as interchangeable, they were regarded as two facets of the highest value, justice.

In Bakunin's theory, the resolution of the interrelationship between these two ideals was greatly facilitated by two utopian presumptions which were to be the basis of the future anarchist order. One was that the future anarchist society would bring economic abundance; the other was that political power would disappear completely. The first presumption permitted the belief that, since resources would satisfy all needs and desires, there would be no need for restrictions and economic discrimination. The second presumption allowed Bakunin to assert that his doctrine of anarchism solved the problem of the inequalities of individuals under the impact of political power. This provided him with the theoretical groundwork for his tirades against Marxism, specifically against the concept of the dictatorship of the proletariat.

> In the name of freedom, which we recognize as the only foundation and the only creative principle of any organization, economic or political, we shall protest against anything even remotely resembling State Communism or State Socialism.[24]

Yet, as we look more closely at Bakunin's formula of liberty and equality, we may observe that the emphasis is definitely shifted toward equality.

> If there is a human being who is freer than I, then I shall necessarily become his slave. If I am freer than any other, then he will become my slave. Therefore equality is an absolutely necessary condition for freedom.
>
> The first duty, the one which we find placed at the top of our considerations, is that of making every effort for the triumph of equality . . . This is the entire program of revolutionary socialism, of which equality is the first condition, the first word. It admits freedom only after equality, in equality and through equality, because freedom outside of equality can only create privilege.[25]

Thus, Bakunin's anarchist society must be uncompromisingly and rigidly equalitarian, since "for the proletariat the smallest inequality is slavery."[26] Yet, both common sense and historical

[24] Bakunin, *Works, Golos Trуda* ed., III, 146.
[25] *Ibid.*, II, 72-73.
[26] *Ibid.*, p. 74.

experience teach us that liberty, in the sense of a wide choice for each individual in determining his way of life, is incompatible with a rigidly equalitarian society.

It may be thought that the spinning of plans for the future is an easy task if these plans are only a body of wishful thinking. The example of Bakunin proves that this is not always the case. At every step of his reasoning, he perceived the difficulties of resolving the problem of liberty and equality. Let us take a few examples. In accordance with his principle of liberty, Bakunin had to acknowledge that everyone had the right to be "lazy or industrious."[27] But from the point of view of equality, he felt himself compelled to introduce a rigid obligation for everyone to work, and to brand those who wished to live without working as "thieves,"[28] leaving them only "the right to starve to death."[29] Again, from the point of view of freedom, Bakunin acknowledged:

> . . . absolute freedom for associations, without excepting those . . . with the aim of corruption and destruction of individual and public freedom.[30]

Such a conception surely leaves no room for a penal system, and Bakunin demanded that it be abolished. But then he found it necessary to discriminate, and in turn reintroduced punishment. Therefore, he provided for the possibility of sentencing individuals who acted against society. Then Bakunin returns to his ideal of freedom, and provides that those under sentence might refuse to submit to its execution. But this was not the end of the matter. Society might in turn exclude such individuals from its ranks and declare them "deprived of all protection." Then, as Bakunin ruthlessly described:

> The refractory one, who has relapsed into the natural law of an eye for an eye and a tooth for a tooth, at least within the territory included in this society, may be plundered, mistreated and even killed, without the society's feeling concerned about him.[31]

If we ask how to define this side of the future which Bakunin postulated, the answer is easy: this would be a return

[27] Bakunin, *Gesammelte Werke*, III, 11.
[28] *Ibid.*, III, 28, 51.
[29] Bakunin, *Works, Golos Truda* ed., V, 201.
[30] Bakunin, *Gesammelte Werke*, III, 11.
[31] *Ibid.*, III, 13.

to barbarism. It may be said that Bakunin was immoral, but it must also be admitted that he was always logical in his immorality. One may reject his assumptions as being contrary to common sense, but from them his conclusions flow with striking consistency.

For this reason, all of Bakunin's humanism is of very dubious value. Although it was stimulated by the most precious and noble inspirations, it failed to realize them. The misery, injustice, and coercion which Bakunin witnessed made him so passionately indignant that he was ready to rush into far worse evils. Bakunin is surely an excellent example of a man whose social and political action was dictated exclusively by what Max Weber calls the "ethic of ultimate ends" (*Gesinnungsethik*), not counterbalanced by the "ethic of responsibility" (*Verantwortungsethik*). The result of Bakunin's approach could only be that depicted by Max Weber:

> . . . if, however, one chases after the ultimate good in a war of beliefs, following a pure ethic of absolute ends, then the goal may be damaged and discredited for generations, because responsibility for consequences is lacking, and two diabolic forces which enter the play remain unknown to the actor. These are inexorable and produce consequences for his action and even for his inner self, to which he must helplessly submit, unless he perceives them. The sentence: "The devil is old; grow old to understand him!" does not refer to age in terms of chronological years.[32]

Bakunin frequently referred to the devil in his speaking and his writing. However, he did not grow spiritually old enough to understand him. This left only one road open to him. He himself described the abyss to which this road might lead.

Safeguards of Anarchist Society

We now proceed to a description of Bakunin's projected future anarchist order. But let us first make a short digression to consider the relationship between Marxism and Bakunin's anarchism in regard to the future social order and the problem of political power. By and large, there is no basic difference between these two doctrines in respect to their final social ends.[33]

[32] Max Weber, *op. cit.*, p. 126.
[33] Cf. Hans Kelsen, *The Political Theory of Bolshevism* (Berkeley, 1948),

But in spite of the compatibility of ends, there is a distinct discrepancy between these two doctrines in the ways postulated to achieve the common goals. Let us repeat that, according to Marxism, a revolutionary mood is brought to fruition by economic development, which gradually and continuously brings ever larger segments of society into decisive opposition to the existing economic and political reality. Conscious indignation is, therefore, a corollary of the economic process. But for anarchism (including that of Bakunin, despite his repeated bows toward Marx's historical materialism), indignation is a revolution-creating factor which must be stimulated into existence at any price. Marxism sees the social revolution as coming inevitably; anarchism believes that it must be made to come, and the sooner the better.

In regard to the problem of political power, let us paraphrase the formulation of Franz L. Neumann. Marxism shares with anarchism the belief that political power is not a natural phenomenon. But Marxism, unlike anarchism, limits the necessity for the existence of political power to a given historical phase through which mankind must pass before the classless society can be established. In contrast with the classic anarchist theory, Marxism finds a remedy against political power in a greater and more highly concentrated political power, which may then be used to smash political power (the stage of the dictatorship of the proletariat). Hence, Marxism takes political power into account up to the moment of the establishment of a classless society.[34]

After that moment, there is an apparent correspondence with anarchist schemes for the future social order. It must, however, be stressed that in Marxist theory the disappearance of the state and of political power is to be strictly determined by the laws of the economic process. The anarchists reject this, and their rejection has important consequences. One is that anarchism is not bound by the laws of economic process in determining the time at which revolution may arrive, but the other is that this doctrine does not and cannot make use of the concept of the withering away of the state and of political power.

Therefore, Bakunin had to declare that "states do not fall by themselves; they can only be crushed by universal, popular, international revolution."[35] At the same time, Bakunin had the sense to realize that, just as states do not fall by themselves, they do have a tendency to be regenerated out of the midst of society. Bakunin did not apply the doctrine of the withering away of the state, and his problem was not finally solved by the destruction of the state. Even this left the new predicament, one no less difficult to resolve, of how to prevent the regeneration of the state. This was of primary importance, since the stateless (and also classless) society is the unconditional goal of anarchism. It is the very essence of its doctrine, that which justified the apparent expediency of anarchist doctrine and the violent tactics of the anarchist movement.

Bakunin tried to solve this crucial problem in various ways. From the whole context of his reasoning, one gets the impression that he believed that all of his proposed measures together, though not any one of them alone, would bring a solution. These were: a) the frenzied destruction of the previous order, b) transformation of the secret society of revolutionaries into a watchdog with the task of guarding against any revival of the previous order, and especially of the state, c) application to the new political structure of society of the greatest possible degree of federalization and by thus parceling out state power, finally annihilating it, d) the total recasting of the economic and productive organization of society, and e) last but not least, the application of an intensive and all-embracing program for the complete reëducation of society according to new principles.

Let us again stress that in his writings Bakunin did not incorporate his ideas into a clear-cut plan. But, considering his general inability to think and write systematically, we should rather be surprised if he had. Therefore, a commentator attempting a critical exposition of Bakunin's ideas must first systematize them. In Bakunin's dispersed statements about the factors which will secure the future anarchist order, we find sufficient support for the outline given above.

As we come to a more detailed discussion of Bakunin's plans for the establishment of a new stateless order, we must interpolate a remark about the role of destruction. Bakunin asserted that the more complete the destruction of the previous order was, the better its return would be prevented, and the more

[35] Bakunin, *Works, Golos Truda* ed., I, 91.

nearly automatically a new, ideal anarchist system would be ensured. He supported this view with Hegelian dialectics, asserting that statism was the thesis, that destruction or amorphism was the antithesis, and that federation would be the synthesis.[36]

It is relatively easy to understand that there would be a direct proportional relationship between the completeness of the destruction of the previous order and the difficulty of re-establishing it. But it is impossible to share Bakunin's conviction that destruction alone could automatically bring any strictly-defined, particular new system. It is another question whether it may be postulated that certain moral and political goals will be achieved because their coming conforms to a causally determined development of the human process. This is an assertion which we shall not discuss. Here, it is enough to say that such an idea does have a logic of its own. This idea is also of practical importance, since it gives an undeniable attraction to political ends which are buttressed by such reasoning.

But Bakunin did not make any clear use of such an approach. He did not attach the achievement of a stateless anarchist order to any causally determined process. He simply asserted that destruction, if only it were complete enough, would bring a stateless society.

There was another aspect of Bakunin's stress on destruction. He was greatly struck by the growing artificiality of modern life and believed that this could be arrested by a radical transformation of the structure of society. It may be remembered that during his period of revolutionary Pan-Slavism, Bakunin had openly advocated the "prevalence of the village over the town, of the rural way of life over the urban."[37] During his anarchist period, such ideas retreated into the background of Bakunin's mind, and he then wished to retain the advantages of the modern industrial process. However, Bakunin still believed that artificiality was bad, and that "nature" was good. He, therefore, believed that frantic destruction would remove that which was artificial, while leaving everything natural, since he felt that that which was natural was indestructible. Thus, destruction alone would bring back a healthy natural condition. Bakunin believed that if only the state, with all its com-

---

[36] Dragomanov, *op. cit.*, p. 512.
[37] Quoted in V. Polonski, *Mikhail A. Bakunin*, p. 31.

partments which separate men one from another, could be destroyed, nature would automatically produce a new and better social organism. This is why destruction plays so large a role in Bakunin's doctrine of anarchism.

Following this line of thought, Bakunin, as we know, advocated the complete and immediate abolition of the state, and not the capture of political power by victorious revolutionary forces. He (at least in theory) condemned any attempt to find a remedy against the political power of the state in the use of political power, as Marxism proposed. He rejected the concept of the dictatorship of the proletariat, and this was one of the causes of his controversy with Marx and his followers. Bakunin's view on this point is clearly fixed in his writings:

> We have already expressed, many times, our deep disgust with the theory of Lassalle and Marx. What it recommends to the workers as the nearest, if not the final, goal is the foundation of a people's state which, according to them, will be nothing other than a dictatorship of the proletariat.
> . . . according to the theory of Marx, the people not only shall not destroy it [the state], they shall even strengthen and consolidate it and then hand it over to the free disposition of its patrons and teachers—the leaders of the Communist Party.[38]
> The state, however much its form may be that of a people's state, will always be an institution for domination and exploitation, and therefore it will always remain a permanent source of slavery and misery. Consequently there is no way to emancipate the people economically and politically, to provide them with well-being and freedom, but to abolish the state, all states, and to do away with, once and forever, everything that is now called *politics*.[39]
> Marxist theory solves this dilemma in a very simple way . . . . They say that such a yoke, the dictatorship of the state, is the inevitable but transitional remedy for achieving the maximum liberation of the people. Anarchy, i.e. freedom, remains the aim; the state, which is dictatorship, is the means . . . . We answer that any dictatorship can have only one aim: self-perpetuation.

[38] Bakunin, *Works, Golos Truda* ed., I, 233, 237.
[39] *Ibid.*, V, 20.

> Between revolutionary dictatorship and the principle
> of the state the difference is only external. In substance
> both are one and the same: the rule of the minority over
> the majority.[40]

Using such arguments, Bakunin rejected the dictatorship
of the proletariat postulated by Marx. Despite their rude
demagoguery, these denunciations contain some logic, since
from the "formalistic" point of view, both the bourgeois and
the proletarian states are "coercive machines."

One may object (as the Marxists did), that such a formalistic definition overlooks the substantive purpose of the coercive
machinery, the content of the coercive order. In the case of
the bourgeois state, it is supposed that its aim is exploitation and
enslavement, while the proletarian state is supposed to produce
emancipation and the smashing of political power. One may also
object that by its own use of the concept of the state, Marxian
doctrine shows that the coercive power which we call the state
may serve very different, even opposite, purposes. (Engel's view
that the state would wither rapidly, since a proletarian state
would need coercion only to suppress exploitation and class
antagonisms, may imply practical consequences, but not theoretical ones.) Nevertheless, the fact remains that if the coercive
power of the state may be used for the smashing of political
power, then it may also be directed toward other ends. Bakunin,
who completely rejected political power and political problems,
had no need to worry about the perplexing theoretical problem,
which is a predicament for every Marxist theoretician, of
explaining how state and political institutions which are supposed to support and reflect a given class structure may be used
to change this structure.

If, however, we consider what Bakunin proposed in his turn,
then he should have been the last to raise objections to the
Marxian concept of the dictatorship of the proletariat. We have
already mentioned that one of the means of preventing the
regeneration of the bourgeois state was to be the watchfulness
of the secret association of revolutionaries. As a watchdog, the
secret organization was to have the duty of guarding against any
revival of the state in the period following the successful revolution. Bakunin never developed this in detail, but the implica-
tions are clear enough. We can guess why the written formu-

[40] *Ibid.*, I, 255-256, 190.

lation was never more than rudimentary, and why even this was concealed in the *Statutes*, which were to remain secret, and in letters to close collaborators. Such proposals were too obviously compromising after Bakunin had taken the stand he did in his controversy with Marx.

In his *Confession*, in referring to his plans during the March Revolution, Bakunin had already written:

> I expected that my secret society would not dissolve itself after the revolution, but that on the contrary it would be strengthened and completed by the addition of all the new active, truly strong elements . . . . I expected that it would supply people to fill the various positions and posts in the revolutionary hierarchy.[41]

In the *Statutes*, which date from Bakunin's anarchist period, he defined the special role of the secret society rather more clearly.

> During and after (as before) the revolution, the members will preserve and consolidate their organization, so that they may replace with their common and combined action any official dictatorship, since that [an official dictatorship] would not fail to lead to the reconstruction of the political, ruling, guardian state.[42]

And in a letter to a member of his secret Alliance, Bakunin developed this idea without reservation.

> Our aim is the creation of a powerful but always invisible revolutionary association which will prepare and direct the revolution. But never, even during open revolution, will the association as a whole or any of its members take any kind of official public office, for in reality it has no other aim than that of destroying all government and making government impossible everywhere. It will give free rein to the revolutionary movement of the masses and to their social construction from the bottom up through voluntary federation and unconditional freedom, but at the same time it will always keep watch so that authorities, governments, and states can never be built again. It will combat all ambition, be it collective (coteries like that of Marx) or individual, through its natural but never official influence over all the members of our

41 Polonski, *Materialy*, I, 209.
42 Bakunin, *Gesammelte Werke*, III, 82.

> *Alliance,* scattered throughout all countries, and it will
> be mighty only through its solidarity of action and its
> unity of principles and aims, which must always be pre-
> served.[43]

According to Bakunin's theory, the secret association was to
watch carefully against the emergence of any authority, and,
thus, to fulfill the high promise of the anarchist creed—the
abolition of the state and of political power forever. This idea
was surely a very utopian one. But if its realization were ever
attempted, it would inevitably turn into an experiment in the
transferral of political coercive power, embodied in official
institutions, away from the center of society and into the hands
of the secret association. Bakunin himself must have grasped,
at least dimly, what the effect would be, for he once stated:
"This is the only dictatorship which I can concede."[44]

If we do not overestimate the importance of Bakunin's
reservation that none of the members of the secret association
might hold any official governmental position (in the *Confession* he had not objected to this); if we suspect that after a
successful revolution the secret society must have lost its strictly
conspiratorial character and limited its exclusiveness to the
scrutinized coöptation of members and a stern adherence to
ideology; and if we recall that, according to Bakunin, the secret
society had to achieve an uncontested political monopoly; then
we have a ready-made model of the phenomenon of the modern
totalitarian party. In this case, coercive political power certainly
would not be obliterated, as it has not been, but strengthened
in its autocratic character. The location of political power is
transferred to a new political formation, the totalitarian party.
The internal rules of the party take on, in reality, the character
of universally obligatory state law. Official state law, losing its
hegemony, may be given value at the pleasure of the party,
or may become a mere dummy. These conclusions stem logically
from Bakunin's postulates. Bakunin's whole idea of making the
secret society into a watchog of the new social order certainly
does diverge from the Marxian concept of the dictatorship of
the proletariat. But it has a great deal in common with the
Bolshevik pattern, in spite of the fact that this has the official
label of "dictatorship of the proletariat."

43 *Ibid.,* III, 103-104.   44 *Ibid.,* III, 99.

Bakunin found another means for the suppression of political power within the anarchist order in the principle of federalism. On this question, he was substantially influenced by Proudhon. However, he went further than his teacher.[45]

The basis for federation was to be provided by the absolutely autonomous commune, "which will always be represented by the majority of the votes of all the adult inhabitants, men and women having equal rights."[46] People who did not earn their living by their own labor were, however, to be deprived of political rights.[47] All officials were to be elected, and their mandates revocable at any moment. This was to prevent the mushrooming of bureaucracy. Local communities organized along these lines were to unite in a free federation of the communes of a province, and in turn, the provinces were to form a national federation. From this a world federation was finally to emerge. Every human individual and every component element of the federation was to have an inalienable right to secession. This federation was also to solve the problem of the stateless nations which were striving for their independence. But the main task which Bakunin assigned to this federalism was that of so parceling out political power that the result would be the total annihilation of the state and of all political domination and power.

Bakunin set up certain preconditions for the success of such a federation. First, existing states can not form the basis for a true federation. They must be totally abolished, and only after their complete destruction can a new federative structure be built. "No centralized, bureaucratic, military state, even if it calls itself republican, can seriously and sincerely enter into an international confederation."[48]

It was another of Bakunin's principles that the building of the pyramidal federative structure must begin with the smallest unit, the commune, and proceed upward. In Bakunin's view, federation was not to be achieved by the bestowing of autonomy on the component parts by a state center. Such federation was, in Bakunin's mind, doomed to failure. Bakunin repeated his slogan of "from the bottom up" so often and with such emphasis

[45] Diehl, *Ueber Socialismus . . .*, p. 125.
[46] Bakunin, *Gesammelte Werke*, III, 14.
[47] *Ibid.*, III, 26.
[48] Bakunin, *Works, Golos Truda* ed., III, 127.

that one gets the impression that here he saw the key to the solution of the whole problem of the future anarchist federation.

And yet, the content of this principle is not unambiguous. Although Bakunin scathingly attacked any "formalistic" schematic concepts, here he relapsed into that very fault. His unconditional reliance on the method of "from the bottom up" was nothing other than a sort of constitutional fetishism, which he denounced so bitterly as utterly inadequate in other cases. And it would not necessarily have provided a solution in his own plan of federation.

Finally, Bakunin stressed that the principle of federalism must not mean the isolation of the constituent federative entities. Since he declared that "unity is the goal toward which humanity irresistibly tends," he found the complicated question of federalism even more difficult. On the one hand, he wished to give the fullest possible autonomy to the component parts; on the other, he desired to secure complete, all-inclusive unity. He was unable to find a criterion for the dynamic equilibrium of centrifugal and centripetal forces in a given federative community. Thus, he declared that:

> The right of free reunion, as well as the right of secession, is the first and most important of all political rights; without that right a confederation would simply be a disguised centralization . . . .[49]

At the same time he said that it is necessary to:

> . . . acknowledge the right of secession of all lands, regions, provinces, communes, associations, and individuals, in the conviction that after the acknowledgement of the right of secession, secession in fact will become impossible.[50]

In addition, Bakunin acknowledged that the "principles of political organization of a land must be the absolute autonomy of the community," and that "every nation, province and community will have the absolute right to dispose of itself."[51] And

---

[49] *Ibid.*, III, 129.
[50] Bakunin, *Gesammelte Werke*, III, 51. A similar view about Soviet federation was once expressed by the eminent Soviet jurist, M. A. Reisner. "In view of the solidarity of the proletariat and of the deep unity of the Communist Party, leading the revolution, any secession from the Union is practically impossible." M. A. Reisner, *Gosudarstvo burzhuazii i R.S.F.S.R.* (Moscow - Petrograd, 1923), p. 380.
[51] *Ibid.*, III, 14, 27.

then he clearly indicates the limitations of this autonomy by saying:

> . . . in order to enter the provincial federation and to become an integral part of a province, it [the community] absolutely must adapt and conform its own constitution to the basic principles of the provincial constitution . . . .[52]

Moreover, the subordinate component parts were obliged to carry out accurately the directions of the superior entities. In case a unit refused, Bakunin provided that it might be excluded and placed outside of any legal protection, and that, if necessary, it might be "brought to reason by the national army."[53] Bakunin acknowledged that the disobedient part had the right of secession. But we have seen that, in practice, secession would be impossible. This sheds a different light on Bakunin's federal structure. Despite Bakunin's verbal incantation of federalism, his whole federative system bore the imprint of prevailing elements of centralization. Indeed, if we may presume that his system were put into practice, it appears that these centralistic elements would completely outweigh the elements of local autonomy. However, this did not dampen Bakunin's hopes that his federalism would bring a full annihilation of political power. Neither did it hamper his attacks on Marx's centralism.

Now we turn to Bakunin's consideration that:

> Political equality is impossible without economic equality . . . . The people realized that the first condition of their humanization must be a radical change in their economic situation.[54]

Here, Bakunin added a new, economic element to the three others which were to achieve the new ideal anarchist future order (the destructiveness of the revolution, the guardian secret society, and political federalism).

However, the doctrine of anarchism, and particularly that of Bakunin, is not an economic one. In general, anarchism deals with economic problems only to the extent that this is made necessary for the achievement of its moral and political aims; otherwise, it leaves them untouched. Above all, this applies to Bakunin. Only out of his interest in securing a stateless society, realizing his ideals of freedom and equality, did

[52] *Ibid.*, III, 15.   [53] *Ibid.*, III, 27.
[54] *Ibid.*, III, 28; Bakunin, *Works, Golos Truda* ed., III, 316.

he pay attention to economic problems in the strict sense. Therefore, it is no wonder that he was content to sketch the broadest
outlines of the future economic system of anarchist society. He
gave a few hints as to the question of production and scarcely
even hints about the questions of distribution and exchange.
How the product is to be shared among those who contribute
to its production is a problem to which he offered no solution.
It is dimly suggested that the wage system will disappear, but
there are no indications of the arrangements which will super-
sede it. We cannot learn from Bakunin's writings whether or
not money will disappear. Once again, we must recall his deep-
seated objection to all prophecy and idle utopian speculation.
This is evocative of Schumpeter's dictum that "the classics of
anarchism . . . avoided errors of reasoning largely by avoiding
reasoning."[55] And yet, one does get the impression from the
sum of Bakunin's reasoning that the production of the future
anarchist order will be so generous, so exuberant, that at last
it will be possible to realize the ideal of the utopians: "To each
according to his needs!"

At the base of his new economic order, Bakunin placed the
following factors: abolition of the individual ownership of
means of production and land, free productive associations of
the laborers, and finally the obligation of all the able-bodied
to work.

It was under the impact of Marxism that Bakunin adopted
the plank of the abolition of individual ownership of capital
goods. But, in his demand for the collective ownership of land,
he was certainly also influenced by the example of the Russian
rural repartitional commune, the *mir*, in which there was no
private ownership of land. The demand that individual ownership be abolished had substantial effects on his sketch of the
future anarchist order. Just as Bakunin's critique of existing
society was decisively influenced by his acceptance of the
Marxian doctrine of class war, so the postulation of the abolition
of private ownership of means of production and of land brought
the final social aims of his doctrine of anarchism very close
to the Marxian goals. By virtue of this, Bakunin became the
founder of the anarchist current which is called communistic or
collectivistic. Bakunin, unlike Proudhon, thought that the aboli-

[55] J. A. Schumpeter, *Capitalism, Socialism, Democracy*, (3rd ed. New
York, 1950) p. 307.

tion of individual ownership was inescapably necessary in order to secure the social equality of all. At the same time, however, Bakunin objected to the Marxian concept of nationalization, according to which the new proletarian state, in the period of the dictatorship of the proletariat, should take possession of all means of production. He demanded that capital goods be given to the workers' productive associations at once. At the moment of the abolition of private ownership, "all capital, the factories, and all the instruments of work and the raw materials were to go to the associations, and the land to those who cultivate it with their own hands."[56]

This was another source of Bakunin's theoretical controversy with Marx. Let us find his objections in a quotation from his writings:

> Like us, the authoritarian Communists [Marxists] seek the abolition of private property. They differ from us chiefly in wishing the state to expropriate everything, while we wish to achieve this end by the abolition of the state and of the juridical rights naturally guaranteed by the state . . . . We must reject this [Marx's] system for two reasons . . . . It is clear that the Marxist system must lead to the creation of a very strong so-called popular government, that is in reality to the domination of an educated minority, which alone is capable of mastering the complicated problems which inevitably must arise with such centralization. Consequently this leads to the slavery of the masses and their exploitation by this intelligent minority.[57]

Therefore, to distinguish himself from the Marxian Socialists, Bakunin called himself "not a communist but a collectivist." This designation was intended to explain that he favored the abolition of private ownership but opposed expropriation by the whole society: i.e., by a new proletarian state.

In Bakunin's view, the solution of the problem of work was to be another basis of the economic anarchist order. Bakunin's attitude toward labor was compatible with that of the whole anarchist tradition, which holds that men prefer to do something rather than to be completely idle, and that, therefore, the work of the world may be accomplished by people fleeing the boredom of standing around with folded arms.

[56] Bakunin, *Works, Golos Truda* ed., V, 197.
[57] Bakunin, *Gesammelte Werke*, III, 117.

One can convince himself of this by submitting to the following experiment: Let him condemn himself for a few days to absolute inaction . . . and toward the end of it he will come to feel that he is a most unfortunate and degraded human being.[58]

Subsequently Bakunin stated:

Divine morality considers work a degradation and a punishment; but human morality sees it as the supreme condition of human happiness and human dignity.[59]

However, Bakunin's discussion of the problem of work never reached the level of a scientific exposition. It merely touches superficially on the problem of man's psychological attitude toward his work and then turns into an exalted praise of labor. Its object was not the technical proficiency of labor; nor was it exhausted by the love of labor. Bakunin hoped and expected that a regenerated labor would furnish something more—an exalted moral system. We have seen that Bakunin took it for granted that the "morals" of the bourgeoisie, nourished by the exploitation and commercialism which permeate the economic and political system, would disappear along with the capitalism with which they were associated. The revolution was to result in the moral regeneration of society, and work was to be the basis for this. Bakunin believed that even before the revolution, under contemporary conditions, the workers showed an incomparably superior degree of moral culture than did the other strata of society. In this attitude toward work, Bakunin's position coincides with the later syndicalist tradition.

Bakunin stated: "As soon as exploitation is abolished, there will be only collective labor in industry, and consequently only collective property." He added: "Individual work will be continued only in intellectual production."[60] It would, however, be risky to try to deduce from this statement Bakunin's ideas on the technical organization of labor. We cannot learn whether Bakunin expected that the division of labor, in the strict sense, would disappear in the anarchist future. What he did stress energetically was that the existing gulf between mental and manual work must be removed.[61] He was very sensitive on this

[58] *Ibid.*, II, 125.
[59] Bakunin, *Works, Golos Truda* ed., IV, 56.
[60] Bakunin, *Gesammelte Werke*, II, 101.
[61] *Ibid.*, III, 20ff.

point and, as we remember, almost considered that the division between mental and manual work formed the basis for the division of society into the classes of the privileged and the deprived. Indeed, probably because of his rural Russian mentality, Bakunin practically equated mental work to leisure. Therefore, he concluded that "the unjust differentiation between mental and manual labor must be changed." How? Here Bakunin was able to give only a very unintelligible answer: "If the learned would work, and the workers would think, then intelligent and free labor would become the fairest claim to fame for mankind."[62] But this rhetoric, apart from confirming the idea that Bakunin believed that the work of a scholar, for instance, is not really work, is too vague to provide a clue to the future arrangement. We might perhaps surmise that in an anarchist society everyone would devote some hours a day to manual work, and rather fewer to "thinking."

Bakunin's rather scattered pronouncements give the impression that what he primarily aimed at was to compel the intellectuals to do physical work.

> But what shall the men of talent, the geniuses, live on? They will live from their collective manual labor like all the others.—What! You want to put the great minds to manual labor, just like the least intelligent?— Yes, that is what we wish, and for two reasons. First, we are convinced that the great minds, far from losing by this, will on the contrary gain greatly in physical health, spiritual strength, and above all in their feeling of solidarity and justice. Second, this is the only way to elevate and humanize manual labor, and thus to create true equality among men.[63]

But Bakunin's main problem in connection with work in the future anarchist society lay elsewhere. We will recall that his social ideals were liberty and equality, and that in conformity to the former, he granted the right to be lazy. For some reason, Bakunin made no clear use of the idea that unearned income would disappear and that, therefore, everyone would face an equal and natural need to work. He assumed that even in the ideal anarchist order it would be possible for some people to exist who, though able to work, did not earn. But the laziness

[62] *Ibid.*, III, 23; Bakunin *Works, Golos Truda* ed., V, 201.
[63] Bakunin, *Gesammelte Werke*, II, 102.

of all would mean the economic death of society, while the regulation of laziness would mean the regimentation of labor and a compulsory obligation to work. This latter was, indeed, required by Bakunin's second ideal of equality. Bakunin untied this Gordian knot in his anarchist theory in the Alexandrian manner, by declaring that everyone had the obligation to work, and by branding those who would not earn by their own labor "social thieves," with only the right to starve.[64] Thus, despite Bakunin's intentions, in his need to find a workable solution, one of his social values was completely swallowed up by another.

Bakunin found another possible basis of a new economic order in anarchist society in the federation of free productive associations. However, his statements on this point are as vague and general as are those on other economic matters. We only learn that the basic units of economic production are to be "workers' associations, industrial as well as agricultural, scientific as well as literary." They were to have the disposition of "all capital, the factories, all the instruments of work, and raw material." They were also to possess all the land. The individual productive associations were to federate, working as always "from the bottom up," creating regional federations of productive communes, national federations of regions, and finally an "international fraternal union."[65]

This appears to be all that Bakunin wrote on this point. There are no clues as to the internal organization of the productive communes, to their membership, to how the product was to be shared among those contributing to its production, to how it was to be exchanged, etc. Bakunin left all these questions unanswered, apparently feeling that his often repeated statement "revolution will do the rest"[66] will fill this gap, too.

> Justice and a social order will emerge automatically from life itself. The state, ceasing to be a Providence, patron, educator, and manager of society, renouncing its punitive authority and being reduced to the function which Proudhon indicated, will become nothing more than a simple business office, a sort of central bookkeeping department, devoted to the service of society.[67]

Thus, Bakunin's economic federative structure corresponded

[64] *Ibid.*, pp. 28, 51; Bakunin *Works, Golos Truda* ed., V, 201.
[65] Bakunin, *Works, Golos Truda* ed., V, 197, 198.
[66] Quoted in Steklov, *op. cit.*, II, 362.
[67] Bakunin, *Selected Works*, pp. 222-223.

to his political one. Although Bakunin never defined the relationship between these two factors more clearly, he presumed
that in the reshaping of society the economic federative organization would make the political one superfluous. The latter
was to absorb the former, and thus, government would be
turned into an "administration of things." This would eliminate
political power in its traditional sense. This Saint-Simonian
idea reached Bakunin through Proudhon.

> Then these local communes will no longer be political,
> as they are today, but economically productive. This will
> become the case when they are freed from any political
> tutelage.[68]

At this point, we should say a few words about the striking
similarity between Bakunin's ideas and those of the later syndicalists. With its principles of class war, the collective ownership of the means of production, its attitude toward work, its
belief in working associations as productive units, its "apolitism,"
and its advocacy of violent action, Bakunin's doctrine of anarchism has all the main elements which also form the basis of
the doctrine of revolutionary syndicalism. It is no exaggeration
to say that Bakunin's teaching is closer to syndicalism than is
that of Proudhon, although Proudhon's direct influence on the
syndicalist movement was much greater than was that of
Bakunin. Therefore, Bakunin's anarchism may be divided into
two branches. With regard to the future anarchist order,
especially in its economic aspects, it approaches syndicalism.
But in regard to the method of achieving the new order (general
revolution, not general strike), Bakunin's method is like that of
Bolshevism. It must be added that Bakunin developed his
scheme of revolution, its program, and its techniques, on his own.

Returning to Bakunin's picture of his future anarchist order,
let us look at the last factor which he postulated as necessary
for the ideal stateless and classless society. This was science,
with education playing a primary role. We should not forget
that Bakunin formulated his world outlook at a time when
natural science had reached the peak of its success. Therefore,
Bakunin's optimism in regard to the possibilities of positive
science was immense, though not, it must be stressed, boundless. He often emphasized the limitations of science.

[68] Bakunin, *Gesammelte Werke*, II, 62.

Science comprehends the thought of reality but not reality itself. The thought of life, but not life itself. This is its limit, its only insuperable limit, since it is grounded in the very nature of human thought, which is the only organ of science.[69]

Bakunin reminded his readers that science would never be able to solve the final riddles of life and nature and stated that if we compare that which has already been discovered with that which remains undiscovered, then it must be admitted that science is still in its cradle.[70]

Yet, Bakunin expressed lucidly his hopes about the future role of science.

Once they [the natural laws inherent in the development of human society] have been recognized, first by science and then through an extensive system of popular education and instruction, once they have become part and parcel of the general consciousness, then the question of liberty will be completely solved. The most recalcitrant authorities will have to admit that there will be no need of political organization, administration, or legislation.[71]

The apparent consequences of such an assumption were far-reaching, for they implied that ultimately, with the advance of science and education, politics and social relationships would become a natural science. As A. Gray neatly phrases it: "Those whose business it is to resolve political problems, if they know their physiology, will look on their difficulties—it comes with rather a shock—as being merely questions in hygiene."[72] This view of Bakunin is rather inconsistent with his more numerous statements on the subject of the limitations of science. Apparently aware of this inconsistency, Bakunin hastened to bury it under rhetoric such as this:

On the one hand, science is indispensable to rational organization. On the other, because it is incapable of dealing with the living reality, it must not be allowed to deal with the real and practical organization of society.[73]

Although Bakunin was so much elated about the role and prospects of science and education, he had to face the pre-

[69] Maximoff, *op. cit.*, p. 70.
[70] Bakunin, *Gesammelte Werke*, I, 109.
[71] Bakunin, *Works, Golos Truda* ed., II, 148.
[72] Gray, *op. cit.*, p. 143.
[73] Bakunin, *Gesammelte Werke*, I, 133.

sumption that this would give an extreme importance and high social position to the savant. This of course hardly concorded with the idea of equality. Thus, Bakunin's praise of science was always coupled with vitriolic attacks against scientists. He called the men of science "a new caste of priests," or more often "a new aristocracy of the intellect." This he called the worst aristocracy of all time, since the aristocracy of birth still possessed to some degree "a kind of chivalrous virtue," and the aristocracy of money "acknowledges that you may have the merits of all the arts, even if it adds: 'But you haven't a penny.'" Bakunin says that while this may still be bearable, the aristocrat of the intellect says: "'You know nothing, you understand nothing, you are a blockhead, and a man of intelligence must put a saddle and bridle on you and lead you.' This is something really intolerable."[74]

Bakunin's philippics against the intellectuals are frequent, and his preaching of the anarchist creed contains much of what must be called anti-intellectualism. This part of his doctrine often reaches depths of naïveté and ignorance and is combined with rough demagoguery. All this comes from Bakunin's fear that the intellectuals would endanger a rigidly equalitarian society. Bakunin wanted to preserve the achievements of science and to create the most favorable conditions possible for its future development—but to do this without contributions from, or without even the existence of, men of science. We find samples of this sort of reasoning in the following abridged passages.

> But if science is to prescribe the rules of life, then the vast majority, millions of people, will be governed by one or two hundred savants. In fact by a much smaller number since . . . sociology alone is supposed to give the happy scholar a profound knowledge of all rules. How many such scholars do we have in Russia, or even in all Europe? Perhaps twenty or thirty men! And these twenty or thirty scientists are to govern the whole world. Can anyone imagine a more foolish and ugly despotism? . . . . If we give them full freedom of action they will start to make experiments on human society, as today they make, for the sake of science, experiments on rabbits, cats and dogs.[75]

[74] *Ibid.*, II, 103.
[75] Bakunin, *Works, Golos Truda* ed., I, 187.

How could this contradiction be solved? On the one hand, science is indispensable to the rational organization of society; on the other hand, being incapable of interesting itself with that which is real and living, it must not interfere with the real or practical organization of society. This contradiction can be solved in only one way: science, as a moral entity existing outside of the universal social life and represented by a corporation of licensed savants, should be liquidated and widely diffused among the masses.[76]

Therefore, there was another problem, one connected with education rather than science, which Bakunin considered as of immense social importance. Bakunin believed that, next to the economic factor, inequality of education was a cause of the class structure of society. He wrote:

As long as there are different degrees of education for the various layers of society, the existence of classes will be inevitable . . . . And if there were to be, to begin with, only a difference in upbringing and education between two classes, this in itself would produce, in a comparatively short time, all the other differences, and human society would relapse into its present state.[77]

From this Bakunin drew the following conclusion:

It follows that society, the entire future of which depends upon the correct solution of the problem of the education and upbringing of children, has not only the right but also the duty to watch this. Society is the natural sponsor of all children of both sexes.[78]

Bakunin's pathetic reliance on education is similar to Babeuf's. Like Babeuf, Bakunin saw one of the roots of inequality in the different education of the rich and of the poor. Indeed, it must be admitted that Babeuf cast a significant spell on anarchism[79] and that this is clearly visible in Bakunin's logic.

We are so convinced that education is the measure of liberty, prosperity and humanity . . . that we demand for the proletariat not only instruction, but the entire course of instruction, total and integral education.[80]

[76] Maximoff, *op. cit.*, p. 80.
[77] Bakunin, *Works, Golos Truda* ed., IV, 49, 43.
[78] Polonski, *Materialy*, III, 128.
[79] Gray, *op. cit.*, pp. 104, 106, 109.
[80] Bakunin, *Gesammelte Werke*, II, 102.

Thus, Bakunin demanded that in the future anarchist society there be a single system of education since he believed that education was as important a factor as economic or political ones in creating social inequality. He felt this the more strongly because he believed that, on the whole, differences in ability were due to differences in education.

In dealing with education, Bakunin showed an exactness unusual for him. He depicted it almost in detail.[81] The following characteristics may be stressed. Education should be unified and the same for all. "The principle of authority . . . the natural starting point . . . when applied to those of tender age" should gradually give way "to increasing liberty." The educational approach should not be a "lax system," but should contribute toward the development of a strong will. Education should not only impart knowledge but also include an extensive ideological training. In addition, "the paternal governments have left the masses to stagnate in an ignorance so profound . . . that it will be necessary to establish schools not only for the people's children, but also for the people themselves."[82]

In line with his revolutionary temper and plans, Bakunin judged that the contemporary bourgeois society lacked the conditions necessary not only for the full realization of, but also for even the slightest attempts at, education as he planned it. In his preaching, the sole task in the contemporary reality was to be the accomplishment of the revolution. This was why he repeatedly called upon the Russian university youths to leave the schools and to go among the people to revolutionize them. This conviction was also the reason for his unfriendly remarks about the resolutions of the First International urging the workers to try to raise their level of education.

Bakunin foresaw the possibility and the necessity of beginning such education only during the transition period, after the successful abolition of the previous social order. "Public education, not fictitious but real education, can exist only in a truly equalitarian society."[83] Bakunin expected some lowering of the level of science in the transitional period.

> It is possible and even probable that in the more or less prolonged transitional period, which will naturally

[81] For a detailed account, see S. Rezneck, "The Political and Social Theory of Bakunin," *American Political Science Review*, Vol. XXI.
[82] Maximoff, *op. cit.*, pp. 333, 334.
[83] Bakunin, *Works, Golos Truda* ed., V, 173.

follow in the wake of great social crisis, the sciences of the highest standing will sink to a level much below that held by each at present.

But he comforted himself by giving an affirmative answer to this question:

What science loses in sublime loftiness, will it not regain by broadening it base?[84]

This manifestation of realism is important not only in itself, but also, and much more so, as an admission that a transitional period will be necessary in the progress toward an ideal social order. Indeed, we learn that this transitional period might last a very long time, in fact that a "few centuries" might be needed until "full social equality would be established upon the earth."[85]

This admission is of extreme importance to Bakunin's whole doctrine of anarchism, for it tacitly concedes that in itself the immediate abolition of the state would not solve the problem of the future order. It implies that, to achieve an ideal reality, it would be necessary to have an extremely long, arduous transitional period of social transformation, one involving the whole society. One may say that such a view is in fact less utopian. But such a view is scarcely compatible with Bakunin's more optimistic anarchist expectations. Indeed, it would appear to shake the foundation of his whole anarchist doctrine, based as it is on the principle of government versus liberty.

Closing Remarks

This was Bakunin's general picture of the stateless anarchist society. It is superfluous to stress that it was also to be a classless society. But we may ask whether Bakunin's scheme of the future anarchist society is really a picture of a society without political domination and without political power, setting aside for the moment the utopian character of such an idea. It is not difficult to answer in the negative. To avoid possible objections to such an answer, let us make a short digression, keeping in mind that the anarchist rejection of political authority did not at the same time mean the rejection of every authority within society.

It is of course true that even in Bakunin's propaganda, and

[84] *Ibid.,* IV, 50.
[85] Maximoff, *op. cit.,* p. 331.

in anarchist practice ever since, anarchism has battled against every sort of authority and legality and has become a mere slogan for lack of responsibility and for the pure power instincts of the masses. And it is true that this grandiloquent and contradictory picture describes what anarchism is in reality, for in its conceptual form anarchism exists only in books. But the conceptual, theoretical form is the object of our exposition, and in its theory, anarchism means not disorder but the lack of domination, a system without political power. In its theory, anarchism not only does not reject, but even includes, the notion of compulsion. What it claims is the possibility of a social change in the nature of compulsion, by virtue of which those submitting to it would not feel it as coercion. The anarchist creed, which wishes to replace official law by conventional norms, still does not wish the abolition of all norms. Let us hasten to add that this correction of the understanding of anarchist doctrine does not make it more practicable, does not take away its utopian character.

It was an anarchism of this sort which Bakunin claimed to represent. Hence, on many occasions, he stressed the need for order and discipline in the future anarchist society. In contrasting the "official action of the state" to the "natural action of a club,"[86] he intended to substitute for official state law a conventional norm like that of a club. He distinguished between the official and therefore tyrannical authority of the state and the non-official and entirely natural action of society on each of its members. He advocated the latter as a goal of anarchist society.

The surprising fact is that Bakunin came very near to realizing that this authority of society itself may be as tyrannical as that exercised by the state. He acknowledged that while the action of society will be more insinuating, less perceptible, it will not for that reason be any less powerful. This assumption shakes the very foundation of his doctrine as based on the simplified formula of liberty versus government, which holds that the state is the sole and unconditional enemy of liberty. Indeed, such an assumption should have induced him to revise his entire anarchist creed since it implies that a man would be delivered from a visible tyrant into the hands of a still more grievous, invisible tyranny. However, Bakunin rid

[86] Bakunin, *Works, Golos Truda* ed., V, 47.

himself of this problem by the simple assertion that "a total revolt against society would be just about as difficult for a man as rebellion against nature."[87] Then, he returned to his passionate obsession, advocacy of revolution.

After this digression, which is intended to show that anarchist theory does not reject every authority as such, we may ask whether Bakunin's doctrine of anarchism does fit into the framework of the postulated anarchist general ideals. We ask whether Bakunin's application of coercive power in the future anarchist society does not overstep the limits of conventional norms and turn into the reintroduction of political power in its traditional dimensions.

We must answer that in spite of its vitriolic anti-state phraseology, Bakunin's doctrine does in fact reintroduce political power and does it on a scale hardly known up to his time. Bakunin's anarchy is not limited to utopian elements. It represents a strange amalgam of utopian theorems on the securing of liberty and non-utopian ones suitable to the conquest of political power and the establishment of the most severe social discipline.

The presence of utopian elements in the ideology of a movement are not necessarily an obstacle to its political victory. "In all great revolutions, utopia has always been the strongest force," says L. Marcuse, adding:

> One will not be deceived by the appearance of these revolutions if one realizes that their dynamics are a blend of two alien, even hostile, forces: one a historically conditioned struggle for power, and the other a supra-historical, age-old and still unwon struggle for paradise. Sometimes both battle-cries are raised by the same persons; from this comes the ambiguity of so many revolutionaries.[88]

This also was the source of the ambiguities in Bakunin as a person and in his doctrine.

In any endeavor to put into practice Bakunin's anarchism, the utopian elements, aimed at the securing of liberty, would not be realizable. The disciplinary elements, left thus unbalanced by other factors, would predominate uncontestably. The culmination would be a total despotism. In this respect, Bakunin's example provides an instructive lesson.

---

[87] Bakunin, *Complete Collection,* I, 15-17.
[88] L. Marcuse, "Vom Wesen der Utopie," *Der Monat,* III, No. 26, 122.

Bakunin's teaching is concealed behind his variations on philosophic themes, and access to it is made yet more difficult by his indolent and unsystematic presentation. Therefore, it has been generally misunderstood. Stress has been placed on the utopian end, anarchy, and not on the technique and methods which the revolutionary movement was to use in its efforts to achieve political power. But the methods postulated altered the potential social ends. Bakunin's techniques could certainly not be considered as a general recipe, which could be used under any conditions. His principles were worked out for application to a particular, historically conditioned, Russian reality. They would work within this reality, and probably nowhere else. At a given moment, all the conditions for revolution which Bakunin postulated met in a conjuncture, and the anticipated result came about. A Bolshevik revolution was needed to expose the true meaning of Bakunin's teaching. The techniques of this revolution were those proposed by Bakunin. Marxism only provided a more attractive label and more reasonable goals, behind which the essence of Bolshevism might hide itself more easily.

In making this statement, we do not intend to say that Marxism was superfluous, nor do we intend to belittle its role in the achievement of Bolshevik victory in Russia. The discussion of this question lies outside the scope of this essay; here we cannot try to evaluate the unquestionably important role of Marxism. Let us remark only that any revolutionary movement in Russia which based its action on the rudimentary ideology of Bakuninism would certainly have broken down. At this point, Marxism was of decisive help.

Masaryk, who was certainly one of the leading Western authorities on the Russian enigma, wrote in his essay, *Sur le bolchévisme*:

> The Bolsheviks have accepted Marxism and pride themselves on being its only orthodox adherents. They do not realize how much they owe to Bakunin, the adversary of Marx . . . . [89]

Perhaps, we may make a small amendment. The Bolsheviks did not need to acknowledge their debt to Bakunin for they had not borrowed his ideas directly. The Bakunin tradition, which had penetrated into every current of the Russian revolutionary

[89] Masaryk, *Sur le bolchévisme* (Geneva, 1921), p. 29.

movement, reached the Bolsheviks almost without their being aware of it. Officially, they might still condemn Bakunin's creed. But of far greater significance than this tradition of Bakuninism was the fact that both Bakunin and the Bolsheviks forged their revolutionary approach in full accordance with the situation which confronted them in Russia.

Bakunin, unlike the Bolsheviks, openly admitted the necessity of adapting the revolutionary pattern to this situation, and it is this which makes it worthwhile to study Bakunin's doctrine. As Masaryk remarked even before World War I: "It is strange how far Bakunin's unrealism coincides with Russian reality."[90]

However, it would be unjust to suppose that the only reason for studying Bakunin's doctrine is the hope of gaining a better understanding of the Russian Bolshevik enigma. As Gray says: "The whole [anarchist] tradition . . . has tended to be neglected by a generation which has laid (we hope) an undue emphasis on Marx."[91] If Gray's statement is correct, and there are many reasons for giving it careful attention, then among the anarchist ideologists it is Bakunin who should attract the first attention.

[90] Masaryk, *Russland und Europa*, II, 35.
[91] Gray, *op. cit.*, p. 134.

Bibliography

Source Material

Bakunin, Michael, *Gesammelte Werke* (3 vols., Berlin 1921-24).

Bakunin, M. A., *Izbrannye sochineniya* [Selected Works], 1 vol., n.p., 1920), cit. Bakunin, *Selected Works*.

Bakunin, Mikhail, *Izbrannye sochineniya* [Selected Works], "Golos Truda" ed., (Petrograd—Moscow, Vol. I, 1922; Vol. II, 1922; Vol. III, 1920; Vol. IV, 1920; Vol. V, 1921), cit. Bakunin, *Works, Golos Truda* ed.

Bakunin, Mikhail A., *Polnoye sobraniye sochinenii* [Complete Collection of Works], (2 vols., St. Petersburg, n.d.), cit. Bakunin, *Complete Collection*.

Bakunin, M. A., *Sobraniye sochinenii i pisem,* 1828-1878 [Collection of Works and Letters, 1828-1878], edited by Yu. M. Steklov (4 vols., Moscow, 1934-35), cit. Bakunin, *Works,* Steklov ed.

Bakunin, Michael, *Marxism, Freedom and the State,* edited by K. J. Kenafick (London, n.d.).

Mikhail Bakunin, 1876-1926, Neizdannye materialy i stati [Unedited Materials and Articles], (Moscow, 1926).

Pisma M. A. Bakunina k A. I. Gerzenu i N. P. Ogarevu, [Bakunin's Letters to Herzen and Ogarev], edited by M. Dragomanov (Geneva, 1896), cit. Dragomanov.

Bakunin, M. A., *Vsesvetnyi revolutsionnyi soyuz sotsiyalnoi demokratii,* [World Revolutionary Alliance of Social Democracy], (Berlin, 1904)

The Political Philosophy of Bakunin: Scientific Anarchism, compiled and edited by G. P. Maximoff (Glencoe, 1953), cit. Maximoff.

Materialy dlya biografii M. Bakunina, [Materials for the Biography of M. Bakunin], edited by Vyacheslav Polonski (3 vols., Moscow 1923-28), cit. Polonski, *Materialy.*

Herzen, Alexander I., *Polnoye sobraniye sochinenii i pisem*, [Complete Collection of Works and Letters], edited by M. K. Lemke (22 vols., Petrograd, 1919-23).

Arnold Ruges Briefwechsel und Tagebuchblätter, edited by P. Nerrich (Vol. I, Berlin, 1886).

Monographs and Studies

Adler, Max, *Die Staatsauffassung des Marxismus* (Vienna, 1922).

Berdiajew, Nikolai, *Sinn und Schicksal des russischen Kommunismus* (Lucerne, 1937).

Camus, Albert, *The Rebel* (New York, 1954).

Carr, E. H., *Michael Bakunin* (London, 1937).

Catlin, G., *The Story of the Political Philosophers* (New York-London, 1939).

Cunow, Heinrich, *Die Marxsche Geschichts-, Gesellschafts-, und Staatslehre* (2 vols., Berlin, 1920-21).

Chizhevski, D. I., *Gegel v Rossii* [Hegel in Russia], (Paris, 1939).

Debogori-Mokriyevich, Vladimir K., *Vospominaniya* [Memoirs], (St. Petersburg, 1906).

Diehl, Karl, *P. J. Proudhon, seine Lehre und sein Leben* (Jena, 1890).

———, *Ueber Sozialismus, Kommunismus und Anarchismus* (2nd ed., Jena, 1911).

Eltzbacher, Paul, *Anarchism* (New York, 1908).

Engels, Friedrich, *Ludwig Feuerbach and the Outcome of Classical Philosophy* (London, 1941).

Gide, Charles and Rist, Charles, *A History of Economic Doctrines from the Time of the Physiocrats to the Present Day* (London-Toronto, 1948).

Gray, Alexander, *The Socialist Tradition, Moses to Lenin* (London-New York-Toronto, 1947).

Grossman, Leonid P., *Spor o Bakunine i Dostoyevskom* [The Debate on Bakunin and Dostoyevski], (Leningrad, 1926).

Hecht, David, *Russian Radicals Look to America* (Cambridge, 1947).

Heintz, Peter, *Anarchismus und Gegenwart* (Zurich, 1951).

Hepner, Benoit P., *Bakounine et le panslavisme révolutionnaire* (Paris, 1950).

Huch, R., *Michael Bakunin und die Anarchie* (Leipzig, 1923).

Kelsen, Hans, *The Political Theory of Bolshevism, A Critical Analysis* (Berkeley-Los Angeles, 1948).

Kenafick, K. J., *Michael Bakunin and Karl Marx* (Melbourne, 1948).

Kohn, Hans, *Pan-Slavism, Its History and Ideology* (Notre Dame, 1953).

Kornilov, A. A., *Gody stranstvii Mikhaila Bakunina* [The Wanderjahre of Michael Bakunin], (Leningrad, 1925).

————, *Molodiye gody Mikhaila Bakunina* [The Youthful Years of Michael Bakunin], (Moscow, 1915).

Kozmin, B., *P. N. Tkachev i revolyutsionnoye dvizheniye 1860-kh godov* [P. N. Tkachev and the Revolutionary Movement of the 1860's], (Moscow, 1922).

Kühne, Walter, *Graf August Cieszkowski, ein Schüler Hegels und des deutschen Geistes* (Leipzig, 1938).

Lenin, V. I., *Religion* (New York, n.d.).

————, *The State and Revolution* (Moscow, 1951).

Löwith, Karl, *Von Hegel bis Nietzsche* (Zurich, 1941).

Lu, S. Y., *The Political Theories of P. J. Proudhon* (New York, 1922).

de Lubac, Henri, *The Un-Marxian Socialist, A Study of Proudhon* (London, 1948).

Mannheim, Karl, *Ideologie und Utopie* (Bonn, 1930).

Marcuse, Herbert, *Reason and Revolution, Hegel and the Rise of Social Theory* (London-New York-Toronto, 1941).

Masaryk, T. G., *Russland und Europa: Studien über die geistigen Strömungen in Russland* (2 vols., Jena, 1913).

Nettlau, Max, *Der Anarchismus von Proudhon zu Kropotkin* (Berlin, 1927).

Nomad, Max, *Apostles of Revolution* (Boston, 1939).

Pfitzner, Josef, *Bakuninstudien* (Prague, 1932).

Plekhanov, I. V., *Anarkhizm i sotsialism* [Anarchism and Socialism], (St. Petersburg, n.d.).

Polonski, Vyacheslav P., *Mihkail Aleksandrovich Bakunin* (Moscow, 1920).

Proudhon, P. J., *General Idea of the Revolution in the Nineteenth Century* (London, 1923).

Reisner, M. A., *Gosudarstvo burzhuazii i R.S.F.S.R.* [The Bourgeois State and the R.S.F.S.R.], (Moscow-Petrograd, 1923).

Slonim, M., *Russkiye predtechi bolshevisma* [Russian Predecessors of Bolshevism], (Berlin, 1922).

Sombart, Werner, *Der proletarische Sozialismus, ("Marxismus")* (2 vols., Jena, 1924).

Stammler, Rudolf, *Die Theorie des Anarchismus* (Berlin, 1894).

Steklov, Yu., *Mikhail Aleksandrovich Bakunin. Ego zhizn i deyatelnost, 1814-1876* [Michael Alexandrovich Bakunin. His Life and his Activity, 1814-1876] (4 vols., Moscow, 1926-27).

Vyshinsky, Andrei Y., *The Law of the Soviet State* (New York, 1948).

Weber, Max, *From Max Weber: Essays in Sociology,* Gerth and Mills, ed. (New York, 1946).

Zenkovsky, V. V., *A History of Russian Philosophy* (Vol. I, New York-London, 1953).

Articles

Billig, J., "Der Zusammenbruch des deutschen Idealismus bei den russischen Romantikern (Bjelinski, Bakunin)," *Archiv für systematische Philosophie und Soziologie,* Vol. XXXIV.

Marcuse, Ludwig, "Vom Wesen der Utopie," *Der Monat,* Vol. III, No. 26.

Neumann, Franz L., "Attitude toward Power," *Political Science Quarterly,* Vol. LXV.

Palmieri, Aurelio F., "A Theorist of the Russian Revolution," *Catholic World,* Vol. CX.

Rezneck, S., "The Political and Social Theory of Bakunin," *American Political Science Review,* Vol. XXI.

Ralli, Z., "Iz moikh vospominanii o M. A. Bakunine," *O Minuv-shem* (A Historic Almanac, St. Petersburg, 1909).

Silberner, Edmund, "Proudhon's Judeophobia," *Historia Judaica*, Vol. X.

Index